The Fullness of
Human
Experience

DANE RUDHYAR

The Fullness of
Human
Experience

*This publication made possible with
the assistance of the Kern Foundation*

**The Theosophical Publishing House
Wheaton, Ill. U.S.A.
Madras, India/London, England**

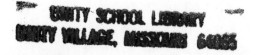

9/03

The Theosophical Publishing House
306 West Geneva Road
Wheaton, Illinois 60189

A publication of the Theosophical Publishing House, a
department of the Theosophical Society in America.

Library of Congress Cataloging in Publication Data
Rudhyar, Dane, 1895- 1985
    The fullness of human experience.
    "A Quest original"—verso t.p.
    Includes index.
    1. Spiritual life. I. Title.
BL624.R793 1986 299' .934 85-40771
ISBN 0-8356-0606-6 (pbk.)

Printed in the United States of America

gift

About the Author

Born in Paris, Dane Rudhyar (1895-1985) was truly a Renaissance man, having gained distinction as a composer, pianist, poet, painter, and prolific author in the fields of astrology, philosophy, and psychology. His creative work was often considered ahead of its time, and his writings show an insight into the trends of the future.

Rudhyar received the Peabody award for music in 1978, and his compositions have been performed in major concert halls. He held honorary doctorates from the California Institute of Transpersonal Psychology and John F. Kennedy University. He is recognized internationally as one of the leading figures in the field of transpersonal astrology and philosophy.

Rudhyar is author of books too numerous to mention, including *Astrology of Personality* and *The Planetarization of Consciousness*. He authored five Quest books including *Culture, Crisis, and Creativity* and the book to which this one is a sequel, *The Rhythm of Wholeness*.

Galley proofs for *The Fullness of Human Experience* were finished before Rudhyar's death on September 13, 1985. In his final talk in March, celebrating his 90th birthday, he said: "The power that held my whole being as a lens to bring ideas to a focus will be released when I go. Perhaps when the person I appear to be is gone, it may be easier to tune up to that mind-power and what is beyond it—the wholeness of spirit, the freed seed."

To Joseph Jacobs

In deep appreciation of his patience
and skill in deciphering and typing the
several versions of this book, and of
his warm response to much of its
contents.

Contents

1

Prelude and Basic Themes

The purpose of this book is to bring to a more concrete and experiential level fundamental concepts of the philosophy of Operative Wholeness, which I outlined in metaphysical form in Parts One and Two of my recent book, *Rhythm of Wholeness*. To fulfill such a purpose, I shall rephrase in more psychological terms some of the ideas previously formulated, and define what is involved in characteristically "human" situations at the level of personal experience, yet without losing sight of the all-inclusive frame of reference, the cyclic Movement of Wholeness.*

Some of the implications of this cyclic structure and the manner in which it should be approached have required a more complete treatment, and the first chapters of this book are devoted to such a process of

---

Rhythm of Wholeness was written in Palo Alto, California, during the years 1981-83. It was published in 1983 by Quest Books, a division of the Theosophical Publishing House in America (P. O. Box 270, Wheaton, Illinois 60189). It contains a Prologue and four Parts: "The Philosophy of Operative Wholeness"; "The Cycle of Being"; "The Cycle of Man"; "In the Spirit of Wholeness."

A previous book, *The Planetarization of Consciousness* (Aurora Press, 205 Third Avenue #2A, New York, N.Y. 10003), was written

elucidation. The concept of structural invariance and the way aleatory developments resulting from individual "free" choices are reabsorbed into the cyclically unfolding pattern of the Movement, will bring, I believe, a deeper understanding of the twin factors of spiritual Compassion and karma. These acquire a new and revealing meaning when related to the ideal of personhood, and the appearance in the earth-field of the Supreme Person—prototype of the state of personhood—at a crucial moment in the planetary cycle. According to esoteric traditions, such a turning point initiated the evolution of humanity and the possibility of radically new types of situations and experiences beyond the compulsions of biological instincts and strictly animal behavior.

In order fully and constructively to deal with the possibilities inherent in human experience, it is necessary to understand the several factors operative in the situations human beings are facing. To most modern minds, an experience implies an experiencer—a "subject" who "has" an experience and therefore is, in some manner, separate from and exterior to it. Such an implication, however, need not be considered valid. The main theme of this book is that this assumption is not valid, even if it is most difficult to avoid at this present stage of human evolution. The basic issue is whether one better understands the process of human evolution in terms of a series of characteristic *situations*, each referring to one phase of the Movement of Wholeness, or according to the old religious scenario in which

in San Jacinto, California in the summer of 1970, after I abandoned several earlier versions, including one in French. An introductory statement of some of the ideas developed in the book was published as a small volume entitled *The Rhythm of Human Fulfillment*, written in 1966 and reprinted in 1973 with some additional material (Seed Center, Palo Alto, California); this small book is now out of print.

spiritual entities (Souls or Monads) somehow emanate from "the One" (God or the Absolute), descend into matter, and eventually, if all goes well, return to their original Home, once more absorbed into the One.

The latter may still be today an almost inevitable interpretation of the type of situations which developed when the strictly human period of our planet's evolution began—thus, when it became possible for a human being to choose between alternative responses to events on the basis of personal desires. Yet this interpretation need not be considered the one "true" interpretation revealing the essential function which humanity can fulfill if it allows the potentialities in its nature fully to develop. What these potentialities actually are can, I believe, be realistically defined only if one understands what is implied in the human condition, definable as "personhood," on the basis of the great cycle to which I have referred as the Movement of Wholeness.

What is to be meant by being a person? Why are human beings today determined to operate as autonomous individuals characteristically able to make responsible decisions? Another question inevitably follows: How does a person arrive at what he or she considers a valid basis for the decision? This basis evidently depends on the particular nature of the choice being made; yet, whether or not the person realizes it, *any* decision implies the acceptance of an approach to life and the meaning of existence which has metaphysical and/or religious roots.

Most religions or spiritual philosophies assume as an incontrovertible fact of inner experiences (particularly in states of intense meditation or ecstasy) that human persons are essentially spiritual entities (Souls or Monads) that, having emerged from "the One" (God or the Absolute), return to their source after a long and dangerous "pilgrimage" through a series of material states. Individuality, and therefore a state of at least relative separateness which allows for basic differences in beingness, are the essential factors in the human condition.

From the point of view of the philosophy of Operative Wholeness presented here and in preceding books, the possibility of making individual choices indeed characterizes the human condition. This possibility acquires its most valid and constructive meaning if these choices are understood in terms of a cyclic series of situations in which many factors are involved. This is in contrast with the responses of individual entities to essentially unrelated events encountered during their mysterious "pilgrimage"—events which happen *to* them, but from which they are essentially separate.

The word *situation* will be more precisely defined in a forthcoming chapter, as will the triune nature of human experiences provided by the series of situations possible at several levels of being. A relatively new meaning will be given to what is to be understood as the "subjective factor" in the experiencing process— one of three factors inherent in such a process at every stage of the cyclic Movement of Wholeness. Before this is attempted, several points implied in the concepts of Wholeness should be clarified: cyclic motion, structural invariance and symmetry, and the relation of spiritual Compassion and karma to the destructuring variations produced by individual human choices. They belong to a substratum of assumptions which cannot be proven or disproven, yet whose acceptance or rejection gives a definite orientation to all human choices, and indeed to everyday behavior and feeling-responses.

One of these most basic assumptions has to do with the universal experience of change common to all human beings. Common as it is, this experience nevertheless can be reacted to and interpreted by the philosophical and religious mind in several fundamentally different ways. The apparent unexpectability of so many of the changes human beings experience may be taken as an indication that existence has an essentially random character, even if the mind is now able to perceive, control and use many patterns of sequential events in terms of cause and effect. Another possibility is implied in the ancient and traditional belief that a changeless Reality, Being or Absolute Principle "is" beyond the multitude of experienced changes, as the source of an ever-present, even if not perceived and understood order. Many philosophers claim that without It there could be no stability or security for the development of human consciousness, and indeed no solid basis for individual or collective choices. A third possibility, however, can be formulated by differentiating *structural processes* from *existential happenings* within the experience and particularly the concept of change. There may be order and structured development within the sequence of ever-changing states of being, but not as the result of the "creation" of that order by a Being transcendent to a world of change and uninvolved in its unfoldment. A permanent inherent structure may be postulated as the invariant foundation of an all-inclusive cyclic series of transformations of states of "being-ness" (the Movement of Wholeness); yet such a structure may allow a great many variations during the human period of the cycle because a third factor is also included which is able to re-establish the temporarily disturbed order.

Such a factor operates in two ways: as quasidivine Compassion and as karma. Understanding both the manner in which the possibility of readjustment may be actualized and the function of the state of personhood in this process is, I believe, of the greatest importance at this crucial phase of human and planetary evolution. In this phase the collective patterns which all cultures have imposed upon the development of human consciousness are crumbling, and so the intense desire to be an "individual" dominates the world-stage.

In the last chapter of this book a suggestion concerning the real nature and purpose of the current crisis will be given, and a brief Epilogue will evoke the ever-present meaning and reality of the situation in a mythic form.

2

Wholeness and the Experience of Periodic Change

The dynamism of Wholeness

When a definable or identifiable boundary can be given to an energy field in which the activities of a number of elements are functionally interrelated, this field constitutes a "whole." The wholeness of this whole results from the coexistence of a state of *multiplicity* (the many elements the field encompasses) and a state of *unity* (the fact that these elements are circumscribed by boundaries). Any boundary-defined field of interrelated activities is thus a particular manifestation of wholeness, regardless of how few or many the number of its constituent elements and how limited or extensive its defining boundaries. Boundaries separate a whole from other wholes, yet all these wholes may in turn be seen as parts of a greater whole containing them all as components.

At the metaphysical level of universally applicable and therefore inevitably abstract concepts, Wholeness may be understood as the interrelatedness of two fundamental principles, Unity and Multiplicity. Moreover, the most common and primordial experience of

7

human beings is that of continual change—a change which may alter to some extent the boundaries of any whole and the nature of the forces active within them which affect other organisms. Therefore, one is led to assume that the relationship between these two principles, Unity and Multiplicity, is also constantly changing. Change implies motion, whether it be the motion of material particles or the development of intellectual concepts. Motion can be observed everywhere and at all times. As Heraclitus stated twenty-five centuries ago, the only thing that does not change is change.

Motion and change may not be at first or superficially perceptible, but the more developed the sensitivity of the senses and the capacity for subtle feeling-reactions and intellectual analysis, the more evident the universality of change. What may at first appear to be a permanent, unchanging entity (or a situation involving several entities) sooner or later is understood as a relatively stable interplay of moving factors and patterns of relationship, which often undergo a rapid or slow series of transformations. Wholeness can only be given the character of a static reality when the primary and incontrovertible human experience of change is dismissed as illusory. But to do so reveals a very basic sense of inner insecurity which the religious or metaphysical mind tries in vain to hide by postulating a changeless Supreme Being who must be transcendent and therefore external to and separate from the world of change which It has created for a purpose no human mind can fathom.

Wholeness is dynamic because it implies motion. Moreover it seems justifiable to give a rhythmic, thus cyclic and repetitive character to this motion. It is an ordered kind of motion. It has a structure—using the word, structure, in its most abstract sense. The feeling-realization of structure emerges from a basic fact of human experience, to which philosophers usually have not given enough attention: the fact that some changes are experienced by a newborn human as having *already* been experienced. This phenomenon of recurrence radically modifies the experience of change. Particularly strong experiences of pleasure or pain, which had focused the attention of the child's organism, are remembered. Some definable change made them happen. In order to understand what the change was related to, and thus perhaps how it could be made to happen again (or be avoided if it was painful), a new faculty begins to develop in the child's organism: *mind.* And mind, as we shall soon see in greater detail, is the ability of an organized whole to discover, invent, and develop a mode of operation—a procedure, strategy, or device—which makes possible the repetition of pleasurable (and in general "desirable") experiences, and the avoidance of painful ones.

Another realization soon follows, which at a later stage of human development becomes crucially important—the realization that the recurrence of a desirable experience can be accelerated *if* the child makes use of the strategy suggested by his or her mind; for instance, by crying in a certain way, or (later on) by imitating parental behavior and doing what they apparently expect.

In other words, the primary experience of a human being is not only that of unceasing changes; it is qualified or modified by two other basically important realizations: the expectable recurrence of certain changes remembered for what they had produced in the experiencing organism, and the realization that what is remembered can be made to occur again, if specific procedures (movements of parts of the body) are followed. Thus there is unceasing change; change is at least to some extent repetitive; and the recurrence can be accelerated or delayed. Because this feeling of acceleration or delay in the satisfaction of vital needs (and later on, ego-desires) becomes an integral part of the child's consciousness as it reacts to everyday experiences, what may be called *the sense of time* develops. It takes specific forms according to the conditions of existence and the needs and wants of the growing child; but it is also basically affected by the attitudes displayed by the family, school, social class, and by the culture having molded their collective responses.

The experience of time

Because the experience of time undertones all other experiences in which change is involved, I shall at once pay special attention to what is in fact implied, though largely not understood, in it. The experience should be differentiated from that of the continuum of change, because while "change" should not be considered as having any beginning or end, "time" as an experience always has a beginning, and it must also end. Between the beginning which was in "the past" and the end which will occur in "the future," a "period of time" extends. The sense of time is not only related to the extension of such a period, but to a subjective personal factor, the desire for some kind of change to occur during that period of time. The speed at which time is "passing" while the satisfaction of the desire for a particular (or generalized and imprecise) change has to be waited for, gives this time-flow a specific character. The waiting for the end of the period may be relaxed or tense; time may seem to pass slowly or quickly.

A peasant who has sown seeds must wait, perhaps while hungry, for the new harvest; the individual student also waits for the results of a test which may determine his entire career. This waiting—a so often repeated human experience—constitutes the experience of time. When referring to it, the psychologist or philosopher speaks of "subjective" time. "Objective" time, on the other hand, deals with periods whose beginning and end are established by external events which a collectivity of human beings can observe and use to define and measure set periods of activity or rest—for instance sunrise and sunset, the full moon, the rise of vegetation in the Spring.

There is actually nothing mysterious about time, except the strange ways in which this basic, common experience of perpetual change has been interpreted. The many interpretations that have been presented by religions and philosophies simply reveal how difficult, if not incomprehensible, it has always been for human beings to have *to wait* for the satisfaction of their desires. The near-impossibility of an "instant fulfillment" of one's desires (the passionate ideal of the hippie generation!) has been translated into the binding power of time; and the fateful nature of this power has been feared, especially with the realization that death ends the period when even the anxiety or anguish (*angst* in German) of waiting no longer exists. Making a god of "Time" and trying to identify one's consciousness with his subliminal nature does not help the situation. Neither does modern science's attempt to divorce time from actual human experience and make it a dimension of the hybrid intellectual frame of reference, space-time. Nor does the philosopher's interpretation of time as an innate category of the human mind make individuals feel better as they wait for the distant fulfillment of their expectations. The division of time into past, present, and future, and especially into "moments," the length of which can be measured according to the collectively accepted schedule of activity of a particular community or nation, is also an ineffectual solution to what should simply be considered and accepted as the basic fact of existence: the succession of ever-changing situations which any organized whole has to meet.

The fact of change implies the experience of succession, or sequence. One sensation "follows" another, even if the first merges unnoticeably into the second. There is continuity when no mental activity has yet differentiated any one experience by relating it to a possible recurrence and a desire for or fear of that recurrence. If two experiences follow each other, one must come *after* the other. This is what is meant by sequence. A series of changes constitutes an ordered or structured sequence of experiences. It is only when these are entitized by the mind as events, having an assumed objective existence *external to* the experiencer, that the modern intellectual finds it possible to juggle pictures or abstract symbols to which a "time position" is attributed. Such a "position" can only have meaning if a starting point for the measurement of objective units has first been established, and the concept of periods of time has developed in the interpretative mind.

The beginning and end of a period are established by what I have called "markers of time." These are normally provided by common human experiences, such as sunrise and sunset, or the appearance of new vegetable growth in the Spring; but every society makes its own markers of time in order to differentiate periods of activity from those of rest. If no period of time—no interval between beginning and end—is considered, only a continuum of changes is experienced. This continuum is, strictly speaking, "time-less"; it does not involve time. Nevertheless it implies the *sequentiality* of experienced changes. It is interpreted by the mind as a succession of events and a series of situations, many of which recur periodically.

Markers of time are special moments. They are the alpha and omega of a series of events or, in the absence of consciously noticeable changes during the in-between "passing of time," of non-events. Moments are changes upon which a subject, waiting or deliberately preparing for the experience of desire-fulfillment, focuses his or her attention. Some of the energy of the whole organism is "tensed toward" what is happening. We can measure the interval between such occurrences, as well as the speed at which they pass and attract the consciousness of the subject during a period of waiting.

A period of waiting may refer to a complex and difficult process of preparation for some final fulfillment. It may be a "test" which must be undergone, a surgical operation to be performed, or a decisive meeting with a would-be lover or adversary. Such a period may seem too brief to the experiencing person, who may then complain of having "so little time." On the contrary, the feeling may be that "too much time" may still elapse before a desired or feared event can occur—so much more waiting has to be endured! If we say that the event occurred "in time," we mean that we had accurately evaluated the interval between that event and the beginning of the process leading to it. We had estimated the value of the interval according to a standard of measurement defined by two markers of time. Our measuring was accurate; but on what basis was the measuring done?

Originally, as far as human beings are concerned, time measurements have always been made on the basis of the experienceability and repetitiveness of situations referring to the dynamic structure of some "greater whole" within whose field of activity the human experiencer operated. That structure provided him or her with standardized markers of time; and by so doing it made possible the measurement of repetitive periods of time having easily definable and commonly acceptable beginnings and ends. The selected greater whole usually was our planet; its daily rotation and its yearly revolution around the sun evidenced a definite rhythm. Other kinds of greater wholes have been used: a religion featuring a series of feast days and centennial periods, the nation whose laws establish periodical recurrences (such as the date of paying income tax), or the schedule followed by a business firm for which a person works. In all cases, by establishing such markers of time in the common experience of a social community, the structure of the greater whole definitely affects the sense of time of the people of the community. It affects their general feeling of having enough or too little time, and of the speed at which this commodity is being spent.

In our Western civilization time is considered an objective commodity of which a small or large amount is available in the interval between two markers of time. We possess such a commodity; it is a kind of wealth or power. The amount which is ours to use can be measured, apportioned, and spent wisely or carelessly according to the vast number of biological needs, socio-cultural requirements and personal ego-wants seeking satisfaction. These wants may appear to be very personal. In fact, they follow a scale of values definitely conditioned and often rigidly determined by a collective culture and religion, and by the example of parents and friends.

The main events most people use for determining the amount of time available to them as particular persons are quite obviously the birth and death of their physical organism, without which no experience would be possible, at least at the present level of human activity and consciousness. Each person's life-span is the period during which the possibility of fulfilling a more or less lengthy series of desires exists. This possibility sets limits to the person's situation, first as a living organism in the biosphere, then as a participant in a sociocultural complex of activities and a partially integrated field of "psychism" (collective consciousness and mass emotions), and finally as an autonomous and self-determined individual-in-the-making in whom a conscious subjective realization of relatively unique and independent identity is developing more or less effectively. The entire life-process experienceable by such a person may lead to the least partial fulfillment of what was possible when birth (or it may be claimed, the impregnation of an ovum by a spermatazoid) marked *the beginning of time* for that particular human situation. Time ends when the marker called death occurs; and as it ends, there is "no more time" in the experienceable sense of the word. One may nevertheless assume that a new situation has emerged from the old. Such a post-mortem situation can be imagined in many ways, and religious and occult revelations have provided a great variety of descriptions.

The great majority of human beings, even if followers of a religion teaching the immortality of the Soul, are never too sure whether what the teaching calls "Soul" actually refers to the gut-feeling of being-I, Peter or Jane; and it is to such a feeling that they cling, terrified of feeling it vanish. The average person all over the world fears death, because he or she is not fully open to the emergence of a new situation in which an as-yet-unknown type of relationship between the familiar factors in their experiences would operate. The unknown is frightening, and entire cultures may be polarized by such a fear. They seek ways of escape, or of prolonging the existence of objective forms in which they tried to condense (as a plant does in a seed) the essential quality of their contribution to the evolution of mankind. Perhaps the most basic desire of individuals or societies is to endure—to deny the inevitability of an end to what, as time, had a beginning.

To refuse to accept this inevitability of death is not, however, to experience timelessness. What is timeless has neither beginning nor end. Change is timeless, just as Wholeness is unlimited by the particularity and dimensionality of any whole. Cyclicity, as we shall see, remains invariant whether cycles are of short or cosmic duration. Death is not the great enemy. The enemy is our binding desire to control and perpetuate ourselves.

Living in the now

The non-existence of time after the period of beingness of *any* whole has ended does not imply the cessation of the continuum of change, or of the succession of situations produced by the cyclic interplay of the two principles of Unity and Multiplicity. This interplay is what human beings perceive as motion, or the dynamic character of Wholeness. Motion implies the unceasing *passing* from one state of Unity-to-Multiplicity relatedness to the next. The word *passing* is stressed because as one deals with the process of change as a cyclic whole (the Movement of Wholeness), one no longer focuses attention upon moments of time, as if they could be separated from one another, but rather upon the sequence of changes. Nevertheless, if one intends to define the exact relation of an experienced event to markers of time in terms of the activity of conscious, autonomous, and responsible individuals, one has to refer to a precise moment assumed to have a specific character. One has to *time* (verb form) actions according to an experienced or required sequence of time-entities (moments) and the possible speed at which the actions can be carried out.

In order to make such a process possible, mind has to interpret the experience of sequence (of before and after) in terms of the quasi-dimensionality of past, present, and future. The individualization of "time units" called moments and made (consciously or not) to resemble living organisms that are born, mature, and die, is undoubtedly necessary when the ego and its desires dominate the human situation. Moreover, at this stage a clearcut distinction is made between an experiencing subject and what it experiences as if it were outside itself. But this is only a phase, however enduring and tenacious, of the human experience of change on which the awareness of existence itself is based. Whether it is the individualization of the continuum of change or that of the state of personhood, individualization inevitably engenders a great deal of confusion and misunderstanding.

The concept of action "*in* the present" is particularly confusing. The reason is that, strictly speaking, the present is only a dimensionless line of demarcation between past and future. It has no more dimensionality than, in geometry, the lines forming a triangle have thickness, or a mathematical point has spatial extension. The present separates the future from the past, but it is also their merging into each other. Where the future meets the past is a very vaguely defined yet extensive moment or series of moments called "now." When philosophers, psychologists and mystics speak of "living in the now," they refer to a more or less brief period of transition which actually has a time-dimension, though it may be characterized as "timeless" because of its special quality as the moment at which the human capacity for decision and action should be focused.

What is meant by "living in the now" (as we are acting or taking decisions) is to be neither affected (or even haunted) by the memory of past experiences—our own and/or those of our ancestors, educators or associates—nor fascinated by an over-idealized and unrealistic subjective longing for a future state, or by an unrealistic fear of what it may bring. It is also to face in a thoroughly awake condition of consciousness, and with focused intent, whatever situation may be just ahead.

The situation has not come; it is not "present." Yet one should be in a constant state of readiness to meet it. For instance, if the driver of a car allows his feelings to dwell upon a deeply depressing past experience of frustrated love, or lets his imagination be entranced by the glowing mistiness of utopian expectations, so that attention is not focused on the road, he may fail to react effectively to the erratic action of another driver suddenly in the wrong lane, and a fatal head-on collision may occur. In this case, of course, the computer-like level of the mind may have been programmed or trained to react automatically in the correct manner. But any training process implies a reference to and use of a knowledge based on collective past experience, and it even includes a certain amount of expectation—the expectation of possible results.

When a modern philosopher-psychologist eulogizes living in the now, he or she actually means meeting life's experiences as an individual being no longer motivated and deeply affected by the way of thinking-feeling-behaving which family and culture had imposed upon mind-development since birth. Theoretically, living in the now should mean being totally unconditioned by *any* past. But one is always conditioned by the past, whether it be the past of the long process of biological evolution which built a human body and its brain, or the past of a people and their culture which provided a language with definite words and a syntax establishing rigid structures of relationship between all the elements of experience. The more intense (as well as traumatic or fame-producing) the events of the first part of a person's life have been, the more impossible it will be for the biological, psychic, and intellectual impressions of these events to be totally eradicated, especially if the person claiming to live in the now has been motivated (consciously or not) by the occurrences to build on them a philosophy of life. The phrase *living in the now* may be a convenient way of systematizing and perhaps glorifying a somewhat self-conscious approach to human existence, stressing the specific quality of a newly activated center of individualized consciousness. Having succeeded to some degree in freeing itself from the binding pressures of culture, and being eager to emphasize the value and excitement of that "liberation"—however relative it may have been—this new center of consciousness is, as it were, mythologizing its feeling-responses.

The basic issue is always the nature or stage of evolution of *who* it is that "lives in the now." Plants and wild animals live in the now, because life "lives them" in terms of its indismissible needs and instinctual modes of response. In his Epistles, Paul states that he is no longer a separate individual entity that "lives," because God "lives him." To many mystics and theosophists, living in the now implies living *in the presence* of God or the "Master." But the realization of such a "presence" should not be confused with what, in relation to past and future conditions of existence, is called "the present." Nothing can be *done* in the present, for the present—I repeat—is only an abstract line separating past from future. Yet it need not be considered a dimensionless line; it need not separate any condition of being, if *the passing*—the moment of being—is experienced as a presence, as the dynamic aspect of Wholeness.

There is motion always and everywhere. That motion is structured, operating as wholes of change, as cycles or eons. Living in the now implies a focusing of the attention of the experiencing subject upon one particular phase of the cycle of change. In the fullest experience possible to a human being, any phase of the Movement of Wholeness is lived in terms of what it reveals of the structure and meaning of the whole eon—thus *sub specie eternitatis*. The moment is lived in the presence of Wholeness. Through it the entire cyclic interaction of the two great principles of Unity and Multiplicity is envisioned.

This interaction operates always and everywhere, yet it is ever-changing. Because variations are possible it is always new; yet, as we shall see, it is also invariant in its total structure because every variation is balanced by a compensatory action. How puny is any "now" unless one can feel in and through it the immense resonance of the whole cycle—the "always and everywhere" of unconditioned Wholeness!

Yet the destiny, function, or dharma of humanity requires both that the expansive power of desires for self-actualization and that the capacity of the mind at the human level to objectify, entitize, analyze, and measure, should experience their fullest possible development in Man. The pressure of the principle of Multiplicity compels men and women to focus their attention upon parts and the mutual interaction of these parts, rather than to resonate to the rhythm of Wholeness in any whole. The same pressure leads the human mind to *dimensionalize* the continuum of change. That

pressure must be obeyed during the phase in the evolution of human culture in which the dominant desire of
the subjective factor in human experience is to express
itself as an ego. The ego is unconcerned with the deep
tide of human evolution because it feels essentially
separate from other individual persons with conflicting
ambitions. Then the human mind has to measure all it
perceives, because it is urged to control the energies
latent in nature for the satisfaction of ever-new desires.

The most crucial and fateful application of the power
to measure is the measuring of time—time now objectivized as a commodity and no longer whole, no
longer cyclically structured; the time of stop-watches
and electronic interferometers and of the abstract
equations of the Einsteinian Theory of Relativity.

Objective time, causality, and the measure of time

The foregoing discussion dealt with the experience of
subjective beings who have desires (or at the biological
level, vital needs) and seek satisfaction of them in and
through situations able to provide it. This satisfaction
has two basic features: the process of fulfillment "takes
time," and it usually involves the concept of causation
—a definite sequence of cause-and-effect, the effect
being the cause of further effects. If the principle of
causality as it is usually understood today is to be taken
as universally true, the categories of "before" and
"after" are also to be given an absolute character. A
cause occurs before its effect. It occurs in what has
ambiguously been called "linear" time. A particular
cause, believed to be past or present, can be expected
to produce a definable future effect.

Thus interpreted, a series of experienced situations

assumes an objective character. Objectivity, however, refers to the fact that a *relation* between the experiencing organism and another entity occupies the mind's attention. A subjective experience, on the other hand, refers to the change directly affecting a whole organism and its centralizing consciousness. When a person is burned by a hot stove in the dark, there is in the experience itself no immediate realization of the stove as a source of heat. However, the mind is called upon to establish both the existence of a hot stove and the precise character of the gesture which brought about the relation between the hand and the stove. Relation generates objectivity. The world around us is objective only because we relate to its many components.

Therefore what is involved in giving objectivity to time—and in a similar sense, to space—is the fact that when consciousness is dominated by mental processes, it deals primarily with relations rather than with experienced changes (events) in themselves. Objective time refers to the succession of changing relations; objective space, to a complex group of "positions" occupied by entities with which a human being can, conceptually if not actually and experienceably, relate himself in terms of measurable "dis-stance" (proximity or remoteness). Whether we refer to objective time or dimensional space we are dealing with *a substratum of relatedness*; that is, with an abstract factor or principle of existence without which there could be no experienced relation. Within this substratum, events occupy positions. The substratum—whether it be space or time, or today in science space-time—contains time-sequences and/or space-positions; but in either case the relations between experienced events and entities are at least partially determined by their distance (in spatial terms) and by the before-and-after succession (in terms of time sequence). Space and time are assumed to be empty containers. As spatial and temporal entities move within the containers, the relations between these entities change; but space and time remain a theoretically infinite possibility of relation. Whether the human mind sees this space and time filled with events or apparently empty, in either case they are abstractions. Their only meaning is as frames of reference which make measurements possible.

If, however, there is an infinite possibility of relations, two of the basic concepts of Western science and of "commonsense" human knowledge, namely, causation and gravitation, may turn out to be neither sacrosanct nor theoretically unchallengeable. Time-sequence may not follow only one cause-and-effect line. The sense of position in time natural for human consciousness may be superseded not only by a much more inclusive fan-like unfoldment of effects, but even by the transformation of the before-and-after sequence. Causation is, of course, an experience common to all human beings; yet today the mind claims the ability to imagine time-sequences not subject to the cause-and-effect (or even before-and-after) sequence, as well as space-relations between masses which would not obey gravitation. In a gravitation-free universe, the concept of physically measurable distance would not be a determining factor in controlling the motion of spacially-determined entities.

If we think of a measurable space *between* entities, or of measurable time *between* the emergence of a desire and its satisfaction, we have to give space and time a definitely *objective* reality. This reality can only have an altogether abstract character, difficult to understand and impossible to experience. It is a construct of the mind which may reveal the natural way for the human mind to operate at this stage of the planet's evolution. The activities of human beings seemingly require such an abstract frame of reference in which events occur and physical masses are located. Events and material objects must have positions in space and time, for without positions there can be no way of measuring *when* and *where* to act. Without one-directional causation sequence (before-and-after), commonsense daily expectability and the scientific prediction of events would be impossible. Such an impossibility would deny any meaning to human efforts at transformation and to moral values, since any act might cause any reaction. For the mind to assume the reality of such a non-ordered situation would be in fact suicidal. Such an assumption would separate mental processes from the experience of being as an integrated whole in a consistently organized structure of situations to which a meaning can be given. This is in fact only possible through the use of words and relations between words divorced from experienceable reality.

The act of measuring is most likely an important part of even the most primitive types of cultural and collective activities. But the principle of measurement in ancient times was certainly not what it is understood to be today in a Western world mentality which, because of the spectacular way in which the principle has "worked," has made it the basis of the only kind of scientifically acceptable knowledge. Not only the practice of measurement, but also the concept of *quantity* as a defining factor in all relations, have acquired—particularly since the sixth century B.C. in East-Mediterranean regions—a rather new and all-pervasive character. What seems to have been a mostly intuitive sense of proportion and rhythm became intellectualized and objectivized by the increasingly precise reference of events to standards of measurement accepted by philosophers and scientists all over the world.

When Pythagoras taught his disciples how to refer personal experiences of tone to a measurable length of vibrating string (the monochord), he may have given the impetus which led the Greek culture to glorify the practice of measuring and the meaning of "proportion." Yet for him, Number and Proportion were not merely abstract concepts but were cosmic principles which could be experienced directly, or at least reflectively. Pythagoras is said to have been able to experience the "Music of the Spheres"; but when he referred to planets and the spatial intervals between them, and to what became known as the Pythagorean scale, he was not thinking of the physical mass of celestial bodies, but of principles of organization of what he already knew to be a sun-centered cosmos (heliocosm).

In ancient Greece the term *intellect* had a highly spiritual meaning, essentially different from the modern use. What was then the "new mind" was a mind of pure relationship and proportion, rationality, and beauty; and its measuring power was believed to be the means to give concrete, experienceable form to cosmic order. This concretized order was the invariant foundation of "the Beautiful." It was only during the fifth and fourth centuries B.C. that an abstract formalism developed, substituting itself for the *experience* of pure proportions.*

The monochord was a rather crude instrument; and so were the sundials and clocks used to reveal the time at which the bells of churches and city halls were rung as vibrant markers of time for a whole integrated community. But as social and business processes became increasingly complex and required more precise

---

*See my recent book *The Magic of Tone and the Art of Music.* Shambhala Publications, 1982, chapter four.

"timing" of exactly when to begin and end a particular activity, time-measuring devices became more exact. They also became individualized, providing for each person his or her own time, thus breaking up the wholeness of personal experience into a series of fragmented happenings.

When changes which affect and to some extent transform an entity (or group of entities) are measured in precise quantitative terms, what is measured has to have an objective character; it is perceived as being external to the measurer. Moreover, the entity in question must have a beginning and, however remote it may be, an end. The process of change being measured should be divisible and commensurate with a previously accepted standard of measurement. While in olden days the standard of measurement necessarily had some kind of relation to the experiences of the measurer—a life-span, certain proportions of the human body, etc.—in modern science the units of measurement, at both ends of the scale of quantitative values, no longer have any experienceable or even rationally imaginable meaning. This leads to the belief that what the atomic scientist and astronomer attempt to measure actually belongs to a level of being which transcends, if not the human condition of existence, then at least the interpretive power of the modern mind. It makes one suspect that the most basic postulate of science—i.e. that "laws of nature" are true everywhere in space and at any time (even at the Big Bang!)—is not true, because the method and perhaps the very concept of measurement apply only to the space "in the neighborhood of" the measurer—which may mean in astronomical terms our Milky Way galaxy, or what the experience of human eyes can observe and directly measure.

One might phrase the issue differently by asking

whether man should trust his mental processes of interpretation rather than his senses. So stated, the issue seems easily answered by the obvious unreliability of human senses in many well-known situations. Yet what is unreliable are the sense-perceptions of *an individual human being*. They are unreliable because they originate not only from one local point of observation, but also from the specific perspective of a particular culture; and perhaps above all because they are affected by the subjective state and the desires (unconscious though they be) of an individual perceiver and experiencer.

The preceding statement, however, should not be construed to imply that anything depending upon a subjective factor is unreliable—though this is the general approach taken by modern Western science. There could be a *unanimous* as well as an *individualized* kind of subjectivity, and I shall deal with the former when speaking of the Pleroma state of being. Indeed, a gradually emerging desire to base collective decisions on a consensus (thus the principle of unanimity) rather than on majority rule has recently become noticeable. This may be not only because of the irrational assumption that the decision of 51% of a people is wiser than that of 49%, but also because of the deep feeling that anything having a fundamental human validity should involve the whole of mankind. It should command unanimous acceptance at the level of subjectivity, rather than in terms of a system of intellectual concepts mathematically proven to be "true." But how could all human beings reach a state of unanimity of desires? How could they *all* have the same desire expressing a unified, all-human subjective self as they are confronted by a fundamental experience implying a crucial choice?

Majority rule and the statistical approach in general are concepts whose validity is evident where strictly intellectual processes operate. They belong to the level not only of formalistic theories, but to the concept of form itself. Modern science has recognized the pitfalls of such thinking by stressing the need for any experiment to be repeatable under varying circumstances for a relative consensus of trained observers and theorists. Likewise, modern democracy since the foundation of the United States of America has more or less reluctantly accepted the existence of self-evident truths and inalienable rights belonging to *all* human beings, not just to the majority or (even less) to a ruling minority. Nevertheless, the powers of perception and the mentality of "trained" observers, as well as the essential beliefs imbedded in a particular culture and the particular conditions of collective existence, do not necessarily have the same character at the level of mind. In human experiences, mind is the interpreter; and interpretation implies a frame of reference which can differ in various cultures. If a frame of reference is to be acceptable to all human beings, it must be based both on the realization that there is a superhuman structure of being underlying the diversity of culture-conditioned collective mentalities, and on the vivid awareness of a more-than-human Being—a "Subject" whose subjective selfhood encompasses in a transcendent manner and unifies all individual selves.

Such a Subject has been given the name of God; and the superhuman structure of being subsuming all natural or cosmic "laws" formulated and formalized by the human mind has been defined as God's Plan of Creation and the manifestation of His Will. This manifestation has a mysterious, humanly incomprehensible and non-rational purpose; but as human beings we are part of it, and we find ourselves existing on a planet whose regular motions provide a sufficiently reliable and effective frame of reference for our sense of time *as long as we relate our desires and our basic activities to its simple rhythms.*

"Natural time" is God's time; and long ago I spoke of it as "God's compassion for chaos." But in a practical, experiential sense it is planetary time. It is time which all human beings have to use as the substratum of their collective and individual feeling regarding the succession of events and the timing of their vitalistic activities. It has to be used until the phase of human evolution comes at which the development of particular cultures challenges, transforms, or deviates from the planetary rhythm of natural time. When our Western civilization succeeded in imposing upon human experience interpretations derived from the rationalistic, analytical and individualizing mind, natural planetary time based on the relation of earth-localities to the sun became superseded by "clock time."

Clock time is a collectively accepted but also an individualized kind of time in which any position of the hands of a clock can be taken as "the beginning of time." In its most characteristic form, clock time is time measured by stop watches, and in a far more sophisticated way, by electronic devices using the speed of light as a basic frame of reference, instead of the sunrise and sunset of planetary time. Clock time, in the most general sense of the term, is the frame of reference enabling human beings—whether in institutionalized groups or as individuals—to *schedule* their actions in order to satisfy their collective or personal desires. Scheduling activity implies dividing time as an available commodity into small individualized entities (moments) whose duration (or length) can be measured and thus given the character of dimensionality. A standard of measure has to be used, and Einstein's revolutionary concepts emerged in the young scientist's mind in answer to a question concerning light—light

whose speed he assumed to be constant and unsur-
passable. Yet for him, light was not meant to be a fact of
direct natural experience (as is the rising sun) but was a
generalized mental interpretation which had been
validated by complex measurements and mathematical
formulae. A system of interpretation—a "theory"—was
formulated in an abstract language based on a frame of
reference (or syntax) in which time is only one of four
coordinates. These four factors are needed to establish
the exact position at which anything can be found and
when any "event" occurs.

The question, "Why should this position be known?",
is very important, yet rarely asked. The answer one
gives has a crucial bearing on the concept of measured
time and on the validity of science in general. The only
realistic answer is that man must know the exact time
and place at which an event will occur *in order to be able
to control it.* To control any process is to exert power over
it for the purpose of using its results for the satisfaction
of a desire. The kind of desire to be satisfied varies, of
course, with the personal or social situation; but the
value attached to precise scientific knowledge in our
present-day world cannot be doubted. It is used to increase chances of survival and material comfort, and in
the conquest of new territory and the utilization of its
resources. This territory is at first physical; but during
the last centuries the conquest and development of a
mental kind of territory, and the control of intellectual
processes involving research, observation, and a
systematized body of interpretation, have become
dominant factors in the evolution of Western civilization.

This is not the place to elaborate a complete theory of
knowledge, but the use of knowledge and the approach
to time are closely related. From a historical point of
view it should be evident that the concept of "knowledge for knowledge's sake," and the belief that all that

is known should be available to anyone, at any time, in any place, and under any conditions, are very new factors in the development of the human mind. In all previous cultures the value of knowledge and the advisability of imparting it have been conditioned by the state of being of the person who would receive that knowledge, and therefore by the expected use this knower would make of it. This use is evidently motivated by the nature and quality of the knower's desires —thus by the level at which his or her subjective self operates—which in turn depends upon his or her state of evolution as a living organism of the homo sapiens type and as a participant in a sociocultural system of organization. Science is usually considered today as the product of a basic human impulse to ascertain more and more facts, and to discover the invariable laws according to which matter, life, society and individual persons operate. But only in our mind-dominated culture is this impulse to know isolated from its basic, even if unconscious, motive: the control of the power which can be released and used in any situation a human being may face.

There are evidently many scientists motivated in their research and their complex intellectual operations solely by what can be rightfully called the "search for knowledge." But it can be so defined because such persons have their consciousness focused mainly at the level of intellectual processes of formulation and (more specifically) formalization. The mind factor dominates their experiences, at least at the level of culture and institutionalized social relationships. They are born to take new steps in the development of the collective mind of their society. It is their dharma; and naturally they give to their (in some instances) obsessive impulse a meaning to which a high social value is attached.

The desire to control is in itself a fundamental

characteristic of the human state. Because human beings can to some extent control the sequence of natural changes and introduce into it unnatural releases of power, they are able to take, *consciously and deliberately*, the next step in the evolutionary process operating within the all-inclusive field of activity of the earth as a planetary organism. And, of course, they may also refuse to take it for a variety of reasons. Human beings are apparently endowed with free will. Free will is the ability to control situations in order to satisfy individual or group desires; and this ability implies the operation of mental processes that provide a technique which can be used to release latent energies— whether biological or social—in order to serve a desired and sustained purpose. The essential factor is the quality of the desire.

The process of effectively and reliably controlling a sequence of changes (or events) requires the act of measurement. As already stated, one has to know precisely where and when the change will take place in order to control it. A frame of reference has to be established in which the elements in an evolving situation which is to be controlled can be accurately defined and exactly located. This is the basic function of calculus. Since Einstein, this frame of reference is generally understood as four-dimensional space-time. In that frame of reference, time loses its subjective meaning. Nothing is being revealed of the motive for control, or of the quality of the experience of *waiting* for the possible actualization of the potential change. The dimensionalizing of time leads to the *experiential* absurdity of "traveling" backward in time, unless one considers the possibility of moving faster than light away from the earth while retaining a human consciousness—which may be just as absurd.

The basic issue always remains the motive for the control of natural processes. To accelerate the evolution of humanity in the direction pursued by the Movement of Wholeness (the great cycle of change) may indeed be a supremely valid purpose if based on what I shall soon define as "Compassion." On the other hand, the desire to control situations for the sake of experiencing, at the level of the ego, a subjective feeling of power and personal or collective pride, inevitably leads, sooner or later, to destructive results. This kind of desire unfortunately is very powerful in the approach our modern civilization takes to time. Behind such an approach is the increasingly feverish multiplication and complexification of desires which the consciousness of the individual person, operating at the ego level of subjectivity, seeks to cram between an immense number of narrowly separated markers of time, and especially of course between the two fundamental ones—birth and death—the beginning and end of measurable time.

Because an over-stimulated mind presents to the ego an unaccomplishable array of possibilities to be desired, there seems to be never "enough time" to actualize them. The more time is measured in small units, the more crowded it becomes, and the more the end of time, death, is feared. Yet if the individualized consciousness could relax into a state of desirelessness and accept the cyclic rhythm of change, death could be but a rite of passage from one level of experiential situations to another.

The fragmented concept of measured time finds its opposite in the realization of the wholeness of time. The isolated moment so rapidly passing, and the anxiety of "not enough time" can vanish or be transcended when the consciousness accepts the cyclic nature of existence. Cyclicity is indeed the dynamic aspect of Wholeness. Always and everywhere Wholeness operates in cycles of motion.

3

The Cyclic Structure of the Movement of Wholeness

Abstract patterns and experienced symbols

When a person's attention is focused upon a repetitive series of common human experiences indicating the working of a cyclic process, three basic approaches are possible: the person may try to live as fully as possible the unfolding, concrete situations as they are being experienced one after the other; the most noticeable events may be given a symbolic character revealing their meaning in terms of the whole process of change; or general principles may be abstracted from the sequence of events, indicating the way the process and all similar ones are structured.

The first approach is experiential and mostly personal, requiring an open and holistic response to each event as it is experienced in itself, with a minimum of attention given to its causes and probable consequences. The second or symbolic approach is concerned not only with the events and the experiences they engender, but also with the relation between these events considered as phases of a whole process. Moreover, it is involved with the meaning of the effects of these events in terms of more or less common human needs or desires, and with the possibility of influencing or controlling these effects. This approach stresses the value of interpersonal communication by means of symbols or myths able to transmit information. The knowledge this information is meant to convey refers specifically to the development of a consciousness of processes, and thus of wholes of experience within definable periods of time.

The third approach seeks to ascertain the structural character of any cyclic series of developments produced by a basic and recurrent situation. It "ab-stracts" operative principles, not so much from the events and the experiences they elicit as from their sequence and essential character. The character is "essential" in the sense that it has a fundamental relevance to situations which in themselves may greatly differ, if only because they operate at different levels of experience. The situations differ existentially, but the *structure* of the process relating the situations is understood to be the same. It is invariant, however varied may be the outer, empirically analyzable events it interrelates. Such a structure can only be discovered through the operation of the human mind when a particular level of mental development has been reached, at least by the intellectual vanguard of mankind. Historically speaking, this seems to have occurred during the sixth century B.C., particularly in India with Gautama the Buddha, and in the Greek world.

The circular pattern indicating the cyclic sequence of phases of the Movement of Wholeness, first presented in *Rhythm of Wholeness* and reproduced here with a few changes in terminology, is the product of this abstract approach. It gives a diagrammatical form to the ever-changing but symmetrical relationship between two fundamental principles, Unity and Multiplicity, which

in psychological terms may be interpreted as subjectivity and objectivity. These principles alternately
wax and wane, producing an oscillatory type of motion.
Neither can ever totally overpower the other. At each
moment of the cycle—in each phase of the entire Movement of Wholeness—both are active, though the ratio
of their power continually changes.

When such a balanced and symmetrical process is
considered, four especially characteristic phases stand
out. Two of them represent the maximum of power of
each principle; and in two others, the principles of
Unity and Multiplicity are of equal strength. Abstract
meanings which have universal applications can be
deduced from the balance of forces which any one
phase of the cycle represents. Yet one has to be careful
not to identify *concrete events* with the state of relation
to which they refer in the abstract diagrams.

When I use concretely observable planetary events
such as sunrise, noon, sunset, and midnight as *symbols*
to communicate the meaning of the most characteristic
phases of a cycle of experiences shared in general by all
human beings on our planet, the approach is mytho-
poetic. A series of common experiences is made into a
myth. The two interacting and moving factors are no
longer such abstract principles as Unity and Multiplicity; they have taken a concrete existential reality—
one might say as light and darkness, or radiance and
material opacity. Both approaches can be combined,
and the abstract pattern may always be considered as
having validity at a "higher mental" or archetypal level.

In this book (and even if less obviously, in *Rhythm of
Wholeness*), I am dealing with *human* experiences. I am
approaching these basic and common experiences, and
the essential meanings they can reveal, by interpreting
the abstract diagram reprinted here in terms of the

largest cycle I am able to conceive in which humanity can be given a definable, workable, and future-oriented meaning. Archetypally speaking, MAN performs a very important function in this cycle, half of which refers to our universe as we perceive it, and the other half to a realm of predominantly subjective being. This mostly subjective half-cycle in which activity is increasingly dominated by the trend toward Unity, is as "real" to the wholes of being (Pleromas) operating during it as our physical and objective universe is to present-day human persons. It is experienceably real, according to the philosophy of Operative Wholeness, because there is no justification for the traditional, absolute opposition between "being" and "non-being," or between the "manifested" and the "unmanifested" aspects of Brahman. The philosophy I present is, as stated in the subtitle of *Rhythm of Wholeness*, "a total affirmation of being." Predominantly subjective being is as real as the condition of predominantly objective being on which mankind is now focusing its collective attention. This attention is now focused on objective being because the human mind is so directed by desires which can only be satisfied in terms of what it calls "matter."

Ancient Hindu psychologists tried to interpret the relation between predominantly objective and subjective modes of experiencing in terms of the common daily human experience of waking consciousness and states of sleep. Four states of consciousness were defined: waking consciousness, dreams still dominated by external events, deep dreamless sleep, and a synthesizing fourth state, *turiya*. It was said that in this last state, subjectivity and objectivity were integrated in a way that most people were not able to experience. I might speak of such a state as the experience of Wholeness—an experience which nevertheless inevitably

AN ABSTRACT DIAGRAM OF
THE MOVEMENT OF WHOLENESS
OR CYCLE OF BEING

States of Predominant Subjectivity (Inistence)

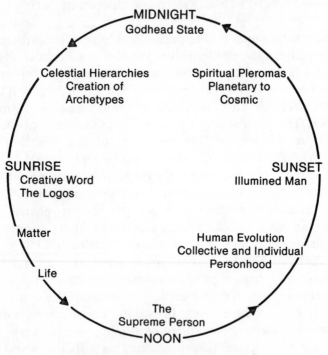

MIDNIGHT
Godhead State

Celestial Hierarchies
Creation of
Archetypes

Spiritual Pleromas
Planetary to
Cosmic

SUNRISE
Creative Word
The Logos

SUNSET
Illumined Man

Matter

Human Evolution
Collective and Individual
Personhood

Life

The
Supreme Person
NOON

States of Predominant Objectivity:
The Material Universe

takes different forms at different levels of being.*

The long period during which humanity evolves from a primitive, strictly biological and "natural" state to that of spiritually "Illumined Man" constitutes the predominantly objective series of phases, which are given a mythical interpretation in terms of the daily cycle of human consciousness on this rotating planet. This is the stage of "waking consciousness." Mankind, in both an individual and a collective sense, has a function to perform. As we shall see in a later chapter, this function can be more significantly understood when interpreted in terms of a relatively new frame of reference, the *Earth-being*, in whose planetary field of activity all human beings participate. Beyond this strictly human and predominantly objective level of reality requiring a body of opaque, light-obscuring physical matter, other levels of being have to be assumed if the whole cycle of being is accepted as the necessary frame of reference.

The superhuman planetary state of being operates in terms of Pleromas of being, whose character and function in the great cycle will soon be discussed. These Pleromas are also "evolving" toward as complete a realization of Unity as possible. They evolve through what is symbolically the deep dreamless state of sleep which leads to the condition of maximum Unity, the Godhead state. This state, of course, has to be considered beyond what human beings mean by the term

---

*The terms *Wholeness* and *Beness* are used almost interchangeably in my works. Every whole is an entity in and through which Wholeness may be realized and experienced. Similarly, every being is a particular manifestation of Beness, a manifestation whose nature and function can be defined in terms of the particular balance of power of the principles of Unity and Multiplicity at that particular point of the Movement of Wholeness. Wholeness is the ever-changing cyclic state of relatedness of Unity to Multiplicity.

"personality" or "personhood." Yet because in such a condition of being, as well as in any other, Wholeness must include the operation of both fundamental principles, Unity and Multiplicity, an experience of the Oneness which would absolutely exclude the drive toward Multiplicity is impossible. In the Godhead, a tremendous surge of Compassion arises which, as we shall see, takes the ideal form of a new universe which will provide a "second chance" for the failures of the past universe to experience Wholeness in a fully re-awakened state.

A new cycle thus begins at the symbolic Midnight hour with the Godhead's vision of what is needed to offset and neutralize the negative memory-remains and waste-products of the old cycle. The envisioned ideal gradually assumes complex archetypal forms, and a moment comes (the symbolic Sunrise) when a tremendous surge of "creative" power arises out of the undefinable immensity of Space—a surge which theologians have interpreted as the Creative Act (or Word) of a God. The Creator may be considered to be one single God, but in that case the existence of this God refers to a unitarian release of cosmogenetic energy. This energy, which we may assume to have a spiral-like character, is soon given a stabilized form; it becomes the potential power inherent in the relatively few material elements to which the chemist gives specific names.

As planets are formed and masses of solid matter react to an immense variety of influences and radiations, "life" begins to appear on the surface of those planets which provide favorable conditions for its development. Symbolically, life manifests during the second half of the period between the Sunrise and Noon period of the great cycle. At Noon a sudden reversal of the cosmic motion occurs. The principle of

Multiplicity having reached the maximum of its power, the principle of Unity once more reasserts itself. A momentous event takes place to which I shall refer as the appearance of the Supreme Person, in whom the cosmogenetic vision of the Godhead finds itself fully objectivized. Then the period of human evolution and the development of "personhood" begins.

These various phases of the Movement of Wholeness, mentioned here in a most condensed form, have been outlined in greater detail in Part Two of *Rhythm of Wholeness*; they will be further analyzed and interpreted in the following chapters Five and Six. Before this can be done in a truly significant manner, a few basic points should be discussed concerning some aspects of the cyclic concept which need special elucidation. The first concept to be clarified is that of symmetry, as the use I have made of the term *symmetrical* can easily lead to some misunderstanding.

The meaning of symmetry

The circular diagram of the cycle of being printed here does *not* always refer to time as a measured factor. When the Hindu *Puranas* speak of periods of cosmic manifestation (*manvantaras*) and non-manifestation (*pralayas*) of Brahman as being equal in terms of years, the statement is relatively meaningless insofar as the pralayas are concerned. Time, as the objective factor to which human beings respond when they measure the speed of changes between markers of time indicating the beginning and end of a period, can have no experiential human meaning when there are no clocks, no moving celestial bodies, no atoms in the process of disintegration to serve as standards of measurement. If a specific length is given to pralaya, conceived as the "non-manifestation" of Brahman, it can only be because one assumes that the states of manifestation and non-manifestation in the whole cycle must be of equal duration. The cyclic pattern is assumed to be symmetrical. But the word *symmetrical* must be given a very broad meaning which suggests "correspondence" rather than what geometry calls symmetry. Symmetry should be understood in a qualitative rather than quantitative and measurable sense. The oscillations of a pendulum are measurably symmetrical, but the development of material and biological systems during one of the four quarters of the circular pattern (from Sunrise to Noon), and whatever is implied in the activity and consciousness of Pleromas in the opposite quarter from Sunset to Midnight, do not have to be symmetrical in terms of measured time. Yet the process of involution—from Midnight to Noon—develops in a manner that can be called symmetrical to that of the process of evolution from Noon to Midnight. Involution and evolution are processes of opposite polarities, and in terms of the wholeness of the cycle they are complementary and symmetrical. The symmetry refers to the structural factor, but not necessarily to existential realities.

One could evidently imagine and postulate that there is no essential structure, no definable order in the series of changes in the relation Unity-to-Multiplicity. Whatever happens and produces the impression of change in human organisms could be interpreted as a random sequence of alterations in the relationship of the experiencing organism to its total environment. Yet the periodic recurrence of many situations characterizing human existence assuredly implies the existence of at least a considerable degree of order. Moreover, the realization that our existence takes place within a field of ordered activities displaying definite (if not always easily definable) structural characteristics, seems essential to the full development of human consciousness. If there is random motion in the universe, this randomness may be attributed to the activity of the principle of Multiplicity; but while always present, it is nevertheless balanced in human situations by a factor of order. Indeed, the essential drive in the constitution, destiny, or dharma of humanity is the attempt constantly to increase the realization of that fundamental order and to give it a wider, more inclusive scope. Such an attempt is collective and takes the form of a culture.

Each culture seeks to define this universal order in a specific way, and to establish a set of structural principles. In most cultures these principles are thought to be the dictates of a creative God; but the classical sciences, which for centuries have dominated the Western mind, speak of these principles of order as natural Law. The term *law* unfortunately evokes the existence of a law-giver; and science has no way to explain how these Laws of nature were imposed upon the release of cosmic energy in a postulated Big Bang. If we refuse to accept the reality of such a causal sequence of Creator and Creation, the bipolar cyclic pattern of the Movement of Wholeness may be considered the Law of Beness. Its structure is very simple and repetitive. As a basic structure it is invariant; yet we do not have to think of that structure as the only factor in the situations we are meeting *as human beings*. Invariance of structure does not have to negate variability in existential relationships, *if* we can also see at work a third factor able to re-establish structural order in the field of existence where it has been disturbed.

This italicized "if" is crucially important, because if such a third factor were not operative we could rationally assume neither a permanent cosmic order (which would negate the possibility of human "free

will"), nor the capacity of human persons to make individual choices (which might irreparably upset the
fundamental order of the cosmos).* This third factor
manifests in two basic ways: as Compassion (*karuna* in
Buddhist terminology) and as karma.

Compassion and karma operate in two basically different ways; the former consciously and deliberately,
the latter unconsciously and compulsively. Through
them, nevertheless, the essentially unpredictable variations and potential disturbances resulting from the
unstructured and unrhythmic desires and activities of
human individuals are reabsorbed into the invariant
structure of the cycle. What was potential in the beginning (alpha) is fulfilled in the end (omega) of the
cyclic Movement of being. The Wholeness of the whole
remains undisturbed in its all-encompassing *structural*
aspect. The disturbances are *existential*; and it is at this
existential level that Compassion and karma operate as
two modes of relatedness between parts of a whole.
They are compensatory, restructuring types of operation through which Wholeness asserts its undismissible
Presence through the momentary and surface modifica-
tions of the essentially and structurally unchangeable
equilibrium inherent in cyclic motion.

Human free will and the process of readjustment

In its most divine aspect, Compassion takes the form of
the Godhead's desire to give to the at least partial

---

*The dilemma has, however, been given a non-rational and
mysterious solution by theologians postulating the existence of a
God who inexplicably creates cosmic laws which even he cannot
break, while at the same time creating human beings free to alter
them though it may mean eternal hell if they do—a hell which nevertheless would not restore the disturbed order!

failures of the past universe a new chance to experience Wholeness fully and concretely. Compassion inspires the vow Bodhisattvas are said to take as they renounce, through immense periods yet to unfold, the supreme bliss of Nirvana in order to be able to assist "all sentient beings" on this planet in experiencing this state of quasi-absolute subjectivity and oneness. This assistance undoubtedly takes forms it is impossible for the ordinary human mind to picture, because they refer to the evolution of humanity as a whole, and indeed of the earth as a planetary being. At a more understandable level of human existence, Compassion can take a multitude of less extensive and radical forms, yet none of these should be confused with merely personal emotions and above all with sentimental feelings. In the Gospels, when Jesus enjoins his disciples to "offer the other cheek" if an angry man has struck them, this kind of abnormal reaction to an experience is intended to be a deliberate, freely made attempt by a conscious and compassionate "I" to readjust the harmony of interactive relationships disturbed by the angry gesture—an act of readjustment being needed to re-equilibrate a situation disturbed by another act of opposite polarity.

An extension of the principle of readjustment is implied in the desires of some human beings to lead lives of asceticism and prayer in order to restore the condition of wholeness thrown out of balance by the lusts and greeds of so many other persons, and indeed made commonplace features of interpersonal relationships and societal organizations. In this religious and quasi-mystical sense, "prayer" means establishing and maintaining open channels of mind and feelings, sustained by biological restraint and the transmutation of life-energies. Through these channels the planet-wide collectivity of transhuman and translucent beings (Saints, Bodhisattvas and true Holy Men) who have transcended the merely human mode of experiencing are able more focally and effectively to release the power needed to balance the unstructured desire for individual freedom, ego-originality, and personal-social attainment inherent in the human phase of the Movement of Wholeness.

On the other hand, *karma* is a restructuring operation which takes place at a cosmic level and restores the invariant character of whole cycles of being by generating conditions of existence (and particularly of physical rebirth) which theoretically neutralize the previous acts or even thoughts of disorder produced by at least relatively free human agents. The original meaning of the word karma seems, however, to have been simply "action"; the implication being that every action produces a reaction, equal but in the opposite direction. This refers, therefore, to Newton's third law of motion, whose application is shown in jet-propulsion, the recoil of guns being fired, and in the results of a speeding car hitting a wall. But when we speak of action and reaction, we should first consider the meaning we give to the word *motion*. Newton's laws of motion imply the existence of material entities moving through space considered as an empty container; but such entities are not directly and originally experienced. The mind of a recently born child gives to a series of recurrent changes, periodically affecting his or her biological organism in a pleasantly or painfully remembered way, the character of entities—a character further emphasized and set by the names attributed to them by his or her family.* Infants and primitive people who interpret

---

*The process of formation of the ego is discussed in my book *Planetarization of Consciousness* and in the booklet *Beyond Personhood* (San Francisco, California: Rudhyar Institute for Transpersonal Activity, 1982). I shall return to it in later chapters.

their collective experiences in animistic terms seem to think of motion as the result of some entity's *actions*. Even at the sophisticated and rationalistic level of classical European thinking, the Creation of all material entities was an act of God who, as causeless First Cause and "Prime Mover," created them "out of nothing" (*ex nihilo*), very much as a dramatist imagines a new situation which he intends to make into a play, but whose development has a will of its own and needs to be watched—a thoroughly anthropomorphic concept!

A much-needed alternative is the idea of perpetual cyclic motion without beginning or end. There is neither beginning nor end in the sense that a whole of motion (a cycle, an Eon) can be made to begin with any phase of the movement. Any situation, as a particular phase of the entire movement, is related to the whole cycle, rather than to an original "mover" or to any other entity participating in the total state of equilibrium of the cyclic motion. An unstructured and at least relatively free action which actualizes an egocentric, unrhythmic desire for comfort, hurried growth, or power, has to be compensated for and balanced by the whole cycle whose structural equilibrium it has disturbed.

Karma does not mean that the person you killed will have to kill you in a future encounter; this would engender an endless series of killings. The disturbance in the Movement of Wholeness, produced by the destructuring and chaotic gesture, has to be absorbed by the whole cycle. It is absorbed positively and spiritually by divine or quasi-divine acts of Compassion. Individual human beings in their limited human capacity can begin to perform such acts. These will be gathered and integrated in Pleroma states of being transcending the human level—states which, at the symbolic Midnight, reach their near-perfect fulfillment in the Godhead.

In other words, karma is the compulsive aspect of the Presence of Wholeness upon a whole that had acquired the capacity to choose between a path of "light" that leads to the full and nearly all-inclusive experience of the Godhead, and the path of "darkness" whose inevitable end is the nearly absolute emptiness and total isolation of an "I" utterly devoid of substance or potency. The latter condition is the opposite of the Godhead state of supreme plenitude; and it can be symbolized by a center without a circle, a mandala without contents, Beness incapable of being. Nevertheless, Wholeness includes the two opposite paths. It also includes the possibility of freedom of choice inherent in the human situation. Because of this possibility, the state of personhood and the culture necessary for its development constitute the critical area of the entire Movement of Wholeness. In the next chapters I shall again consider the meaning of this human phase of the whole process of being.

It is hard to conceive how the invariant structure of cyclic being can be maintained under the conditions of perpetual variability which the human situation makes possible. One has to postulate the operation, through Compassion and karma, of a metacosmic power able perpetually to readjust all disequilibratory individual actions generated by human desires and individual free will. The myths of many religions provide a guarded explanation of various ways in which such a process of reabsorption (or karmic neutralization) takes place. Classical Greece believed in the actually unimaginable work of the three Fates (*Moirae* in Greek, *Parcae* in Latin) continually weaving the ever-changing patterns of interpersonal relationships and intercultural events; a blind procedure, for no human consciousness could possibly envision the quasi-infinite complexity of the meshing of more or less individualized lines of readjustment. The unmeasurable number of crossings of event-lines, which not only every human being but humanity as a whole, the planet, the solar system, etc. lives through as experienceable situations, cannot be interpreted adequately in terms of what is now popularly known as "synchronicity." What happens as an apparently significant coincidence (significant to some individualized mind) at a "moment" isolated from the entire cycle of time is not the important fact. The entire meshing of destinies within a whole of balanced motion is involved.

We can, of course, establish boundaries separating the line of readjustment of an assumedly individual and unique person, Peter or Jane, from the lives of other persons; but if we do that, we in fact isolate what we take to be the cause of a series of effects from the complex group of desires that emerged from the subjectivity factor in Peter's or Jane's experiences largely as the result of their relatedness to family, culture, and the whole planet. A particular phase of the Movement of Wholeness comes to a focal point in Peter's karma-producing experiences and responses. But if this "Peter" in fact turns out to be the student who, by murdering the Austrian archduke in Sarajevo in 1914, led to World War I, to Hitler, and the immense and fateful changes in human civilization and the earth's biosphere which followed as effects of that precipitating cause, what kind of individual karmic retribution could possibly readjust such a "free" action? The student should indeed be considered a focusing instrument for the destructuring of our Euro-American civilization. The "effect" of his act has to be met by the whole of humanity. In religious Christian terms, not only humanity is involved in acts of such momentous importance; the collective karma of mankind, extending as far back as an "Original Sin," within them calls for the compassionate sacrifice of God's Son (an ever-present "atonement"). In terms of such a frame of reference, the Fatherhood of God symbolizes the invariant structure of the Movement of Wholeness—the cyclicity of any particular cycle. Divine Sonship is the forever readjusting power that absorbs all disordering personal or collective human desires into the tide of a supreme manifestation of the Love that is pure Compassion.

Christ asked his disciples to radiate at least a reflection of that divine Love in meeting other human beings. The Greek term *agape*, so badly translated as "charity," refers to what human beings can experience of such a divine Love. But when Christ enjoined his disciples to "love one another," he added the far less often quoted words "as I have loved you." Christ-love, like the *karuna* which wells up from the heart of the Bodhisattvas, is that power whose operation makes it possible for Wholeness to remain a constant Presence while, at the human level of evolution, the principle of Multiplicity challenges the rise of the longing for Unity through the seeming "freedom" of personal desires. But such desires are still deeply affected by the memory of biological urges. Can one really speak of freedom; or does one not rather witness, in so many instances, the operation of unfulfilled karma?

For the individual person, the choice is nevertheless open. He or she may accept the karmic confrontation and the *full* implications of the situation confronting the individual—thus restoring Wholeness and re-attuning oneself to the rhythmic flow of the Movement. He or she may also repeat once more the ancient disturbance and deepen the need for future karmic impacts, unless a power of Compassion is able to act within and transfigure the situation.

If, however, we think of *individualized* karma, we have to accept the idea of "something" to which this karma clings and can be transmitted from one biological organism and personality to the next. This "something" has been understood in two basically different ways: as an individual supernatural and spiritual entity that periodically reincarnates, or as a set of "imprints" which karma-producing desires, thoughts, and acts have made upon a postulated substance or substratum of being (often referred to as "astral light" or "akhasa"). These imprints condition the formation of the structure of a new body and personality, giving it the possibility of either erasing the imprints or deepening them through repetition.

The first way of dealing with the problem of karma-transmission is most generally accepted by anyone believing in reincarnation.* The karma-affected spiritual entity may be thought of as a God-created individual Soul, as a perpetually existent monad, as an *atman* essentially identical to the universal *Brahman* though appearing to be an individual entity. The alternative solution has been most clearly advanced by Gautama, the Buddha, in his *anatma* doctrine, and the transmitted karmic imprints are known in Buddhism as the *skandhas.* The concept introduced by the philosophy of Operative Wholeness is closer to the latter interpretation than to the first. It may indeed be very close to what Gautama might have said if he had not deliberately avoided any metaphysical speculation. Instead, he solely concentrated on the basic situation concretely evident in the lives of human beings, without relating it to pre- or post-human phases of an all-inclusive cycle of

---

*For an in-depth discussion of the concept of reincarnation, see *Rhythm of Wholeness,* chapter eleven.

being.* He apparently was solely concerned (at least in
his public message) with the healing of the suffering-
producing stresses (*dukkha*) he saw inherent in the
human situation. Perhaps an alternative approach is
possible which, by integrating the human situation
within an all-inclusive cycle of being, gives it a more
acceptable and exalting meaning by presenting it as a
necessary transition—indeed a prelude—to a more-
than-human condition, the Pleroma state.

If one imagines a metaphysical, mystical, non-
existential condition transcending the human situation
in an absolute sense, and if one speaks of it as perfect
Bliss or subliminal ecstasy, it seems obvious that what
is evoked has to be understood as the opposite of whatever one has felt to be limiting, imperfect, and a cause
of suffering, anxiety, or impotency in one's life as a
human being. The God of most theologies has, in a
perfect and sublime condition, all the qualities a human
person longs to have but does not possess. A state of
consciousness called mystical may give a human being
who has concentrated upon and visualized images of
perfection and unchanging bliss the subjective feeling-
realization that he or she has reached such a state for
what seems a timeless moment. But it is a subjective
state, and no *human* situation can occur that would give
it the character of actually changeless permanence. In
order to reach it, other factors in the situation—implied

---

*Nirvana does not refer to a future post-human phase of the
Movement of Wholeness. Instead, it seems to have implied either
a state of total identification with the cyclic Motion, or the absorption of the individual consciousness into the wholeness of whatever greater whole within which it had been operating. Such
an absorption is made possible by the "extinction" of the desire
for individual existence. But the Buddha seems never to have
discussed publicly what such an extinction leads to, except in
the very general and comforting sense that it is unalloyed
"bliss."

in the personhood of the mystic—have to be not only devalued, but in a very real sense paralyzed. The resulting situation thus is no longer "whole." A feeling-experience of unification or oneness may be reached; but as we saw, the principle of Unity is only one of the two components of Wholeness. Can we or should we try to deny any reality to the principle of Multiplicity? If we do, the very possibility of "being" is denied. But then "who" is it who denies? The very act of denial is an affirmation of beingness.

What is fundamentally at stake is the interpretation given to the human situation in general—and secondarily to any particular and personal situation being experienced. It is a question of whether or not one somehow assumes that the experience is *outside* the situation which mind—one's own mind—interprets. But nothing can "be" outside the Movement of Wholeness. What "is" may be a step in the direction of "light," or one in the direction of "darkness." But, as noted earlier, both directions are implied in Wholeness, just as Unity and Multiplicity are inherent and inseparable factors in any whole. Nevertheless, from a strictly human point of view, the ideal of encompassing Unity is closer to the idea of Wholeness than the evident fact of the multiplicity of cells in the single body of a person. These many cells can be separated from one another; yet if separated they die as cells (thus as units of organization) unless a biologist, by giving them food— the energy potential in material aggregates—maintains their beingness as units.

Indeed, human evolution is the gradual process during which the "Presence" of the principle of Unity becomes an ever more powerful factor in the most basic situations. These, however, operate as vast currents in the oceanic depths of being; they allow storms to agitate the surface of the water. The power of the principle of Multiplicity, no longer *externalized* in a multitude of slightly different biological features, is *internalized* in typically human situations. This may take the form of ambition and hunger for power and wealth of a multitude of egos—as the craving of an artist for originality, of a scientist to be the first to make a discovery, or of a mountain climber to reach the peak of Mount Everest. All these expressions of the cosmic drive toward Multiplicity are essential parts of the general human situation. No one facing any personal situation should ignore them or minimize their importance and power.

A psychology and an ethics of Wholeness have to be based on the inclusion of *all* factors in any situation. A metaphysics of Wholeness must take into consideration and encompass every possibility of relationship between the principles of Unity and Multiplicity—including those in which one of the two principles is *nearly*, but not quite, all-powerful. A religion of Wholeness should include God within the cycle of Wholeness (in whatever form this Presence may be conceived or felt) as one of these extreme states of being; and Man and Nature should be included as well. Such a religion also should not shrink from the realization that God must have a polar opposite, and that the fullness of experience possible for the Godhead has to be balanced by the devastated emptiness of whatever is represented by the condition of nearly absolute Multiplicity.*

---

*The term "emptiness" as used here must not be equated with the type of emptiness or voidness which the Buddhist term, *sunyata*, conveys. The human experience of nearly total emptiness, as well as the mystic's Dark Night of the Soul, are situations of crisis of transformation which require radical denudation and a deconditioning process. This is a transition between two levels of experiencing. It implies transmutation of fundamental desires and, as we shall see in the next chapter, also a new level of subjectivity.

Total inclusion is the unavoidable attitude of whomever understands and is ready, willing, and able to apply the concept of Operative Wholeness to any situation with which he or she is confronted and accepts to live through and endure.   This is an extremely difficult attitude to maintain. If what it implies is clearly understood at an intellectual level, the acceptance of any situation at an emotional level will be made easier. An effective basis for such an understanding should be found in the realization that human situations cannot be fully met in terms of the old psychological and metaphysical dualism of subject and object. An awareness of the triune character of experiences is needed to establish a fully conscious, constructive and inclusive relationship between the factors, whose simultaneous operation alone may reveal the significant place any situation occupies and the purpose it serves in the development of the individual person.

4

The
Human
Situation

The Movement of Wholeness as
a cyclic series of situations

In this book the word *situation* is given a very broad
meaning which includes yet transcends its ordinary
use. A situation is one of the many possible ways in
which a phase of the Movement of Wholeness is
actualized. The character and inherent quality of that
phase refers to a particular relationship between the
dynamic polarities of being, Unity and Multiplicity.
I speak of a "situation" whether the principle of Unity
or the principle of Multiplicity is dominant; thus,
whether that situation occurs in a physically objective
universe or in a mostly subjective realm of being that
may be called "divine." The Godhead state is a situation; so is the life-span of a biological organism. And
the activity of Celestial Hierarchies (the various aspects
of the divine Mind) produces a multitude of situations,
just as does the organization of human beings into
tribal communities or large cities.

Any situation, when apprehended and given meaning in terms of the structural relationship of the

56

forever-interacting two polarities of Wholeness, should be considered threefold. The two principles of Unity and Multiplicity operate in it respectively as an integrative and whole-making, and as a fragmenting and differentiating, trend. But their dynamic relatedness assumes the character of a whole in the situation. Unity and Multiplicity operate always and everywhere as interrelated and interdependent "presences"; and Wholeness—which also means relatedness—is an implied "third." Furthermore, Wholeness implies consciousness.

Consciousness is inherent in any whole because the word *consciousness* is another symbolic way of referring to the relatedness of the Unity and Multiplicity factors in any phase of the Movement of Wholeness. Every phase represents a level of being; and consciousness at that level assumes a characteristic *quality*. This quality is inherent in the type of situations activated and made to operate at that level of Unity-to-Multiplicity relatedness—thus, of Wholeness. There may be many situations of that type, but they all refer to and make explicit the potentiality of development of this specific quality of consciousness.

Thus, the operation of an elementary kind of consciousness has to be assumed even in the condition of existence which the human senses perceive and mind interprets as matter; and the biological and functional activity of cells within living organisms reveals consciousness at work at a higher level of complexity. A still more inclusive type of consciousness finds expression in the symbols, the capacity for interpersonal cooperation and co-conscious transmission of information characterizing all full-grown human cultures.

As levels of organization and activity are reached which transcend personhood and local cultures, and as one acknowledges the existence of spiritual and predominantly subjective communities (Pleromas of quasi-divine beings), the possibility of a type of consciousness that surpasses human understanding also has to be accepted. The immensely inclusive and radiant quality of such a consciousness presupposes states of being of which stars and galaxies may be the material representation, because the modern mind is no longer willing to think of celestial gods. Human consciousness may be able to *reflect* such transcendent states of being, as the calm surface of a lake may reflect the full moon. But it is a symptom of a rather naïve *hubris* to believe that the consciousness of a person operating strictly at the human level of body-materiality and of biological, sociocultural organization can do more than reflect "divine" modes of consciousness. At the root of such pride one can readily find a deep sense of insecurity.

The nature of this insecurity which characterizes the human condition can easily be understood. One has only to realize that, while at the biological level of sentiency and compulsive instinctual reactions, consciousness had been operating in situations in which the species-as-a-whole was the subjective factor, this factor begins to assume a personal character with the appearance of truly human beings and human situations. A process of individualization begins which leads to increasing difficulties and to the rise of anxiety in the consciousness of whomever it affects—and eventually this means every human being.

The first stage of the process is the development of particular cultures in and through which a group of human beings gives organized and ritualized forms to their togetherness and cooperation. But out of this collective and hardly more than biological type of organization, the intense desire in human beings to emerge as "individuals" who are able to demonstrate free will becomes a driving factor in human evolution. The process of individualization generates strong tension, emotional stresses, interpersonal conflicts, and therefore insecurity. Religion and philosophy are called upon to heal this insecurity and to lead to numinous experiences of Wholeness. Different doctrines are made to fit the specific needs of various types of insecure human beings, and in the process what had been the subjective factor in a whole biological species becomes condensed and particularized in a human subject whose consciousness, as a result, takes an individualized form.

During the prehuman phases of the Movement of Wholeness, mind acts in situations developing in the earth's biosphere for the purpose of focusing into the concrete shapes of physical bodies archetypes created by the celestial Hierarchies—each archetype having a specific function in the operation of the planet as a whole. When the "bottom" of the great cycle of being is reached (the symbolic Noon) the principle of Multiplicity is as compelling as it ever can be. A reversal of the Movement of Wholeness occurs, and a new type of living beings (homo sapiens) appears. The beginning of a truly "human" evolution is made possible by the gradual rise to power of the principle of Unity; but besides the activation of a new archetype another factor is also implied. The ideal or celestial *form* of MAN-Anthropos manifests in the field of activity and consciousness of the earth as *a Being*. I refer to such a Being as the Supreme Person, because *when concretely actualized* in a "body" of earth-substance, the archetype assumes characteristics which, in their totality, constitute the state of *personhood*—provided we use the term in its most essential meaning.

The Supreme Person is the prototype of personhood. In *Rhythm of Wholeness* I referred to "It" (as such a state

of being transcends gender) as the original or great
Avatar. Under whatever name, It is the "Solution"
which had been envisioned by the Godhead in the
symbolic Midnight as an "Idea" or a formula of relationship, now concretized in material objectivity. The
idea is no longer only a form, but a "Presence"; and this
Presence has power, for in It the sublime Compassion
of the Godhead is pulsating. It is Wholeness operating
in "substance." However, the kind of substance which
could be an adequate substratum for the concrete
actualization of the supreme vision of the almost totally
subjective Godhead state inevitably has to be a substance of a quasi-spiritual kind. The substance of the
"body" of the Supreme Person can only be the subtlest,
most unified matter available within the earth-field.
The normally developed human senses cannot perceive
such matter; and the energy latent in such a "body" is
so intense that it would destroy all natural human
organisms. Esoteric students assume that this kind of
matter-energy appertains only to the highest "etheric"
sub-planes (sixth and seventh) of the physical world,
while what we perceive as solid, liquid and gaseous
matter refers to the first, second and third sub-planes—
the fourth (fire) and perhaps the fifth (more specifically
mental) are related to all radical transformation and
personal metamorphosis.

In a subsequent chapter I shall consider more fully
the meaning of the Supreme Person and the influence
It has upon the evolution of personhood and of humanity as a whole. I should nevertheless state here that the
effectiveness of the prototype of any instrumentality
intended to bring about the large-scale transformation
of whatever it is to replace can only be demonstrated
when this prototype is reproduced in a large number of
specimens of the same type. The Godhead's Solution
proves adequate and successful to the extent that the

personhood of the Supreme Person will be replicated in many human persons as yet to evolve. These beings, now ready or karmically impelled to experience the human state, had known varying degrees of failure in the past—or from another point of view, are the heirs to the "karmic residua" (or *skandhas*) of ancient failures. Replication here, however, is a complex process, because just as failure can take an immense variety of forms, so the "redemptive" process of Compassion and karma must be adjusted to each category of persons and events. The Supreme Person, therefore, has potentially to embody an extremely complex Solution.

The human situation implied in the concrete application of this multilevel Solution to a myriad of specific types of failure must also be immensely complex and differentiated. Moreover, it has to be worked out at the various sublevels of a strictly human kind of substantiality—thus, in terms of the actual experience of human beings operating at different stages of the evolutionary process. The process of karmic redemption or neutralization requires the development in earth-time of a long series of cultures, in some cases operating simultaneously on different continents. Each culture presents a limited collective kind of solution befitting the basic needs of persons born in the society, or even more specifically in one of its particular classes or religions. Each group has its own collective desires and expectations through which it has to face its karma and work its "redemption." A culture is inspired at the core of its collective being (its "psychism") by one of the basic aspects of the immensely complex Supreme Person. This one particular aspect becomes the spiritual source of the culture. It embodies itself in a secondary kind of Avatar. Such a limited avataric personage is also a prototype, but a prototype of only one particular culture. The specific quality of his or her emanation, the symbolic life-events and teachings of the Avatar, serve as a model to the persons evolving through their participation in that culture.

The replication of the achievements of the avataric person or seminal group can, however, occur in two different ways—or rather, at two levels of transmission of a new principle of organization. One may call this transmission esoteric or exoteric; but it is more realistic and significant to speak of a private and public transfer. At first, up to a certain point in human evolution, a private and personal (yet in another sense trans-personal) transmission is the only possible one. A person who has succeeded in achieving his or her radical metamorphosis selects, privately instructs, and transmits to a chosen disciple of his or her "Ray" (or characteristic line of "redemption") the Solution he or she had also received in privacy and secrecy. But the procedure may also be *public*, at least to a large extent. In the latter case, basic concepts and procedures are formulated in a verbal, actional or illustrative and ethical manner. Great avataric beings like Gautama and Jesus made public what they had either at least partially been taught in ancient sanctuaries and through traditional practices, or had gained through intuitive, suprasensible and metalogical contacts with their already developed higher mind, or with Pleroma beings who helped them to understand the deeper objective meaning of their experiences while on the Path.

I shall return to the meaning which can be given to the polarization of the symbolic Midnight/Noon phases of the Movement of Wholeness and its relation to the Supreme Person. I should nevertheless state here that this polarization constitutes a situation in which the most extreme values of the polar trends toward Unity and Multiplicity can be integrated. Their integration is the supreme manifestation of Wholeness because in it the tension between Unity and Multiplicity reaches a degree of maximum intensity. The stresses this tension produces in the Movement of being are the greatest possible. This maximum of tension and stress characterizes the human situation. It is the foundation required for the development of what is ambiguously called human "free will"—the capacity to choose between alternatives.

Several possibilities of action or thought may be possible, yet ultimately there are two basic alternatives: on the one hand, the way that is attuned to the increasing power of the principle of Unity after the Noon point of the cycle; and on the other, the way which resists that increase and clings to the desire for an ideal of individual or group power. The first alternative leads to what may be termed spiritual "success" during the human period of the great cycle of being; the second, to at least partial failure.

In most cases, failure means not having been able fully to apply, in terms of concrete existential events and decisions, the particular solution envisioned by the Godhead and formulated by the celestial Hierarchies with reference to a specific set or collection of karmic deposits when a period of choice in the person's (or humanity as a whole's) life-cycle comes to an end. In a planetary sense, this crucial moment after which no fundamental choice is possible has been symbolized as the separation of the sheep from the goats. This process of separation does not refer to a final "Judgement," since many superficial improvements may still occur. But a no-longer-modifiable limit is nevertheless established, which defines what is possible to whatever has evolved so far.

When one tries to understand and to accept or reject—partially if not totally—any situation, the *possibility* of transformation is the basic factor to consider.

The subject ("I," the individual who assumedly has the capacity to choose) may desire a radical transformation, and mind may present various procedures or a specific and formalized technique to achieve what "seems" to be the "heart's desire"; but neither desire nor technique can become concretely and substantially actualized unless a third factor adequately operates. This factor is *potency*. The power to perform the action which has been chosen has to be latent in the situation. It is not latent only in the subject considered as an entity in itself, or in the mental processes formulating a possible method of achievement; yet it is potentially related to both the subject and the mental factors. The three factors are interrelated in the new experience.

To assert that an individual meets a situation and exists apart from it in a mysteriously subjective yet conscious manner is confusing and unrealistic. A subject does not "have" an experience which the particular situation elicits. The subject is an integral component of the situation, and does not essentially exist outside the experiencing. Each new or old situation, each experience implies a subjective factor which belongs to it, just as it implies the operation of mind-processes and the release of kinetic energy—i.e. of the power to act. Every experience is triune. The Movement of Wholeness is a cyclic series of situations giving rise to experiences to which the subjective factor of desire gives a particular purpose, and the operation of mind a particular meaning. But these experiences must, first of all, be possible. Purpose and meaning require the possibility of fully experiencing the situation—any situation.

A holontological view of human experience

In ordinary use, the word *experience*, whether as a noun ("My wife had a wonderful experience") or as a verb

("I experienced much pain"), implies an experienc*er*.
"Someone" in a particular situation "had" an experience. The situation gave rise to or produced an experience affecting the consciousness and the state of
wholeness of *a* being. This being existed as an organismic whole before the situation occurred which
affected him or her as experiencer. Though he or she
may be affected by what took place, the experiencer is
believed to retain his or her identity *outside* the situation
which gave rise to the experience. What is considered
"the same" situation may be experienced differently by
several entities, each reacting to it in a particular
manner according to his or her nature and character.
Likewise, the same person may be assumed to have different experiences arising from different situations. In
all cases the fact that an experiencer considers an experience as "his or her own" implies the seemingly
incontrovertible feeling of existing outside the experience, even if the latter deeply modifies the state of
being with which the experiencer had until then
identified himself or herself—his or her self-image.

From the point of view of the philosophy of Operative Wholeness, and also according to the *anatma*
doctrine constituting the foundation of Buddhist
thought (at least in its public aspect), no situation is
ever the same. There is likewise no experiencing subject having a separate permanent being as an *atman*
outside the situation he or she experiences. Situations
always change, and so does the subjective factor inherent in them. In ancient Greece, before Parmenides
apparently introduced the dualistic notion of being
and becoming—a notion which has plagued Western
civilization ever since—Heraclitus had asserted that
no one crossing a river at different times experiences
the same water. But in the same century, the Buddha

taught in India that the person who at different times enters the ever-flowing stream is also not the same person. All situations, understood as successive phases of the Movement of Wholeness, are different. Each phase of the relationship between the principles of Unity and Multiplicity makes a different type of situation possible. But because the principle of Multiplicity is active, one type of situation may produce a great diversity of experiences in a variety of environmental conditions—each environment or ecosystem containing numerous living organisms able to experience the situation. However, in order for an organism to experience, the wholeness of the whole has to focus itself. It has to become at-tentive (i.e. to develop a state of "tension toward" an imminent or already unfolding situation). *The consciousness aspect of wholeness must condense itself into a subjective factor in the experience.*

This subject may either accept or refuse the experience. The refusal of an experience, however, engenders a negative situation which in many instances eventually has to be harmonized by the operation of karmic "tensions" needed to compensate for or neutralize the previous lack of "attention." The deepest roots of karma are indeed the result of what is *not done,* rather than of a disruptive action. The most basic failures are the failures to act when a situation presents itself as the new phase of the cycle of being which demands that an unfamiliar step be taken.

The refusal to act and to experience may have one of two fundamental causes: the memory of a similar experience which had been oppressive, painful or frightening, or a feeling of impotency producing an expectation of failure. In the first case the memory factor has its source in mind. This may be the mind of the individual person faced by the situation and remembering one or more similar events, or the collective mind of a culture, a particular religion, or social class that impressed forcibly upon the personal mind a doctrine or a particular way of life which excludes numerous possible responses to rigidly defined situations. In the second case, the lack of attention (or even more, the sense of not being able to rise to the occasion) has its roots in some organismic lack—thus in an ineffective presence of Wholeness, and (at the biological level) the absence of vital energy.

Consciousness, as an operative aspect of Wholeness, condenses itself into a subject when an organized whole *accepts* to experience the confronting situation. Acceptance may be based on the memory of a similar experience which gave pleasure and enhanced the power of expansion and self-multiplication inherent in the biological and psychic whole. Acceptance may also be motivated by an exuberance of power, whether at the biological level or that of sociocultural relationship with other persons or with a social environment.

At the prehuman and strictly biological level of evolution, the possibility of acceptance or refusal does not exist insofar as a *particular* plant or animal is concerned. The subjective factor resides in *the whole* species rather than in any of its specimens. Any specimen is indeed expendable. The survival, welfare and expansion of the species as a whole is the only important (or at least the essential) motive. If an evolutionary mutation is required, it takes place in the seed. The seed belongs to the species, not to any particular specimen. It is a genetic factor, even if the mutation is induced in the species-as-a-whole by the experiences of some particular specimen (or a group of them) having been confronted with and successfully meeting a radically altered life-situation. Only at the level of truly "human" situations is a basic choice possible on an individual basis. Even at that level, for a long period of human evolution, the individual character of the choice is only a latent possibility. It is latent within the collective structure of beliefs and ways of behavior which any culture imposes upon a child from birth, and which he or she has to unquestioningly accept. Indeed, for years the child has to operate *within* the collective matrix of the culture and the societal way of life almost as compulsively as a foetus within the biological womb of the mother. His or her individuality is only a potentiality.

In order to operate as an "individual" in relative freedom, the child (or in traditional societies, the adolescent) has to detach his or her subjectivity from the *collective* subject which had for many years dominated and in most cases still largely dominates the latent subjectivity factor in his or her experiences. The detachable character of the subjective factor in the experiencing of a situation is indeed the fundamental feature of the human situation. There must be detachment not only from the containment and limitations of the cultural and family matrix (operating in terms of the collective psychism of the society and its particular cults, religion, and integrated group-behavior) but also from the usually even more compulsive power of biological instincts. Both types of "liberation" are essential if true individual selfhood is to develop, and its desires and will are able to become controlling factors in human experience.

A third kind of liberation is necessary at the end of, as well as throughout the process of transformation called "the Path," if the super-individual state of Pleroma is to be reached. It is a liberation from the desire to retain a consciousness of separateness as an individual, where *separateness* means the desire to act according to "my own pleasure" rather than as the evolution of the whole of humanity demands. Acting in terms of the evolutionary need, not only of humanity but the whole planet considered as the Earth-being within which mankind fulfills a definite function, is not what is usually called "altruism." Altruism is a horizontal kind of relationship. The relation of the narrowly focused and individualistically defined person to the "greater whole" represented by the Earth-being and particularly by the Pleroma constitutes a vertical type of relation.

I have dealt with the distinction between horizontal and vertical relationships in *Rhythm of Wholeness* (Part Four, chapter twelve). I shall return to it briefly in chapter six when more fully explaining the meaning I give to the term Earth-being, indicating in broad terms the quality of subjective desires which impels an individual person to accept the long and arduous process of metamorphosis leading to the humanhood-transcending Pleroma state.

At this point, the basic fact which must be stressed in the approach to experience I am presenting is that three factors operate in all experiences. The subjectivity factor is only one of the three. The subjective realization of selfhood—even the subtlest I-feeling—is not essentially external to the experience which a particular situation engenders; yet at the human level of existence, what comes to believe itself the experiencer of the experience has had the power to detach itself from the wholeness of the experience. The experience as a whole is triune. It affects and to some extent changes a whole of being; and for this reason I speak of the "holontological" way of understanding experience (from *holos*, whole and *ontos*, being). In every phase of the Movement of Wholeness, "being" can experience its fullness. But the level of the experience and the scope and quality of the consciousness of fullness of being differ at every stage of the cyclic process. As the factor of subjectivity changes, so also does the manner in which the formative mind operates and the nature of the power whose release makes the experience possible.

In current usage, the word *experience* is in most cases restricted to the level of activity and the consciousness of human beings. The experiencer is a "person," Peter or Jane; and the experience involves the three above-mentioned factors: a subject, a mind, and a body able to release power through biological processes. Yet usually, and even in a philosophical and religious sense, the subjective factor in the series of daily experiences a person calls his or her life is somehow singled out and identified with the whole person. This person knows himself or herself as "I." But can there be an "I" without an experience, if we give the word *experience* its largest meaning? Nevertheless, we are accustomed to give to experience a narrow significance. We reduce it to the human level at which personhood develops; we identify the subjective factor in "our" experiences with the whole person of which we assume "I" is the independent and at least essentially transcendent subject—in religious terms, the individual Soul. The result is, I believe, a fundamental kind of psychological confusion, unavoidable as it may be in a period of transition between two levels of being.

In the next chapter I shall attempt to show how the operations of the three basic factors in experience can be at least broadly or abstractly envisioned throughout the entire cycle of Wholeness. We shall then be better able to give to *personhood* its fullest and most essential meaning. It has such a meaning in the Supreme Person whose appearance in the field of existence of the Earth-being occurs at the symbolic Noon of the Movement of Wholeness when the rise of the principle of Unity begins. Yet this prototypal meaning will only be realized in the fullness of human nature on a transformed earth, when the human cycle ends and the Pleroma of the Perfect—the seed remnants of our humanity—pursue their evolution in a realm of being in which the drive toward a state of all-inclusive Oneness increasingly yet never absolutely overpowers the trend toward Multiplicity.

5

The Three Factors in Experience and their Cyclic Transformations

Subjectivity and desire

In the preceding chapter the factor of subjectivity was shown to result from a condensation of the Wholeness of an organized whole whose attention had been aroused by a developing situation. This whole is organized, in the sense that it is based on and structured by a particular value and quality of the cyclically and symmetrically unfolding relationship between the principles of Unity and Multiplicity. This whole thus operates as one of the many manifestations of a particular and definable phase of the Movement of Wholeness. A great number of such manifestations occur because during the half-cycle when the state of being assumes the character of an objective universe, the drive toward self-multiplication and differentiation dominates all situations.

These existential situations take place at several basic levels of operation. The most primary level is the one which human beings interpret and relate to as "matter"; and the concept of materiality refers to a type of motion structured by patterns of interatomic and molecular activity. The next level is that of biological organization and organic function to which the ambiguous name "life" is given. At the level of strictly human situations, the state of personhood is gradually unfolding a set of far-reaching and radically transformative potentialities. These become actualized within the field of societal systems in which a powerful and compelling collective psychism develops. Cultures are formed, mature, and disintegrate.

Each level of organization activates a particular aspect of Wholeness, and consciousness is an inherent component of Wholeness. In any whole operating as part of a functionally effective larger planetary or cosmic system, a particular type of consciousness is at least latent. Consciousness passes from the state of latency, or of only diffuse presence, to that of focalized operation when a situation with which the whole is not conversant arouses its attention.*

What I call the subjective factor in an experience expresses itself as a positive or negative desire for the experience. The term desire, however, should be given a meaning much broader than its common use, even in psychology and religious philosophy. As I stated in *Rhythm of Wholeness* (chapter Five, p. 155), the word *kama* (desire) originally referred to the great *Kama Deva*, the first of the gods because he represented the divine desire to be, which led to the creation of a new world. In early Greek mythology, Eros was also the primordial god in whom this supreme desire was activated. I have interpreted such a desire as the infinite Compassion of the Godhead—the highest, most sublime manifestation of the subjective factor in any experience.

---

*If there is no arousal of attention we speak of partial or total indifference. A particular type of indifference has been called "spiritual" because it refers to the non-operation and transcendence of the kind of desires related to the ego.

This subjective factor nevertheless operates in any experience and at all levels of being, even if we do not use the term *desire* to refer to the subjective factor. At the level of matter, this subjective factor operates in elemental modes of activity we perceive as atomic and molecular attraction and repulsion. In living organisms, desire has a functional organic character, where will manifests as instinct. But as the new relationship between an ascending trend toward Unity and a slowly retreating principle of Multiplicity makes possible and increasingly stresses characteristically human situations, a new type of desire gives an unprecedented character to the subjective factor in the experiences: that of an ego.

The ego, however, is not only a subjective factor, for its aim is to make a newborn and growing human organism as comfortable as it can be, and to satisfy its biopsychic desires as much as possible within the family and social environment in which it has been born. The ego is therefore a kind of compromise between what the innate biological temperament of a growing child and adolescent needs, and perhaps even more wants, in order to actualize its full potential of being, and what family traditions, religion, culture, and a particular kind of interpersonal relationship often relentlessly demand. Yet the ego should not be considered only a composite aggregation of habits, characteristic reactions, and more or less rigid patterns of feeling; it is also the first manifestation at the *human level* of the subjective factor in the process of experiencing any situation.

This human type of subjectivity has the already mentioned capacity to detach itself from the experience. Because it has become a detachable factor, subjectivity assumes an at least relatively exterior character with regard to the whole situation the human organism is facing. The subjective factor that was inherent in all material, cosmic, or biological situations before the appearance of homo sapiens in the earth's biosphere becomes the subject "having" the experience. The difference is crucial, and I believe it cannot be adequately understood unless it is given meaning with reference to the long period of the Movement of Wholeness representing the entire evolution of mankind, and to the function and purpose this evolution fulfills in the entire cycle.

When the subjective factor in an experience assumes that it is *the subject of* the experience, what is experienced becomes *the object* being experienced. Once the dualism of subject and object is definitely and unquestionably established as the "reality" of the human situation, a great variety of consequences follow. They characterize conscious behavior, personal feelings, and the way in which the subject refers and relates to the biological organism he or she calls "his" or "her" body. As the new attitude toward experiencing is defined, interpreted, and formalized by the mind factor, the subject speaks of "his" or "her" mind. This mind has come to confuse the evolutionary state of personhood with the experiencing subject.

The state of personhood is a stage in the cyclic unfoldment of the Movement of Wholeness. So are matter and life—matter as a stabilized condition of energy, and life as a type of material organization able to maintain, expand, and somewhat modify the scope of its activity through replication and sexual procreation. Personhood, however, has a crucial significance because in both its essential and ultimate meanings it represents the concrete actualization of the Solution which the Godhead envisioned during the symbolic Midnight phase of the great cycle of being. This Solution, then only a potentiality, is now totally infused with and dynamized by Compassion. Personhood should likewise be permeated and radiant with at least the reflection of this divine Compassion. It is so pervaded when it manifests as the Supreme Person who appears on this earth at the "bottom" of the cycle (the symbolic Noon). Personhood is also filled with the same divine Compassion when individualized persons, who have become "perfect" through the metamorphic process often called the Path, in their togetherness constitute the Pleroma—the seed and foundation of a series of states of quasi-divine radiance. Though beyond personhood, these can only be attained *through* personhood. No step can ever be missed.

Personhood is a stage of the cyclic process of being during which human situations are to be experienced. But these situations should be experienced with the whole of the experiencing being, and not with a being divided into subject and object. More significant still, in a realistic sense, is the similar division into a wielder of power and the power being wielded. The body is useable power; it is energy condensed into material (molecular and organic) structures, each of which has its function in the organismic whole. That energy has to be liberated into acts through muscles or through mental processes. Desire is the liberator, but the process of liberation depends not only upon the will which focuses the desire (as a lens focuses diffuse sunlight) but first of all upon mind. Mind is the technician that provides effective procedures enabling the subjective factor in the experience to relate to and act upon an available and adequate source of power at whatever level of operation is needed.

Desire and the will it mobilizes are ineffectual if operating alone. The activity of mind has to be included in the process. However, if the desire-projecting subjective factor assumes that it is essentially exterior to the situation which could fulfill the desire, it has to depend upon mind and its techniques in a way which not only distorts or vitiates the direct spontaneous release of the needed power but also gives intellectual and analytical procedures a compelling authority. Sooner or later the entire situation takes on a disharmonic character. The subject may be deeply frustrated by his or her experience, just because he or she believes it is "his" or "hers." No experience can ever be full if it is "had" by a subject essentially exterior to the experience.

What psychology today calls the ego is a subjective factor in experiences in which an evolving person tries to come to terms with parents, partner, the cultural environment, and with the body that is the essential source of power. This is the case until a radical transmutation of desires has occurred. The ego is the first manifestation of subjectivity at the human level because, with the development of collective cultures, the generic power of instinct is no longer fully adequate to deal with increasingly complex and changeable situations. Cultures are matrices for personhood. Just as the embryo begins to act as a foetus when it kicks against the maternal womb placing boundaries to its growth, likewise when a baby rapidly developing as a person on the basis of his or her particular biological temperament starts to feel frustrated in the satisfaction of his or her desires by the family "don'ts" and cultural taboos, the subjective factor in experience calls upon the mind to find procedures which could lead to desire-satisfaction in spite of the "don'ts."

The sum-total of these procedures, and their repetitive features, constitute the ego. To the parents they define the "character" of the child, which may be "good" and easy to handle, or "bad" and difficult. What the parents usually fail to realize is that they are not referring to the child alone, but to a family situation in which they are active and determining participants. The child's ego is an answer to the total situation; it does not develop outside the parent-child relationship. It is only that part of the evolving personhood which refers to the possibility of effecting a change in a frustrating situation. When, in spite of the more or less devious or dramatic procedures suggested by the mind and generally manifesting as muscular acts like crying or smiling, the situation does not change, the subjective factor—tense with repressed desires and perhaps the memory of physical harm—*detaches itself* from the family situation. What the psychologist Fritz Kunkel called "the breakdown of the We-consciousness" occurs. The shocked and distraught subjective factor in the experiencing child seeks and is able to disengage itself from situations it cannot change. Situations still occur, but they now seem to occur *outside* a rather mysterious entity, the subject. This subject first becomes identified by the name given to the child by the parents and the peer-group; but in a still more basic sense it is "I myself." In this assertion, the subject as "I" proclaims its being as separate from and exterior to all situations.

In previous writings I have referred to this process of detachment as the process of individualization. It can only operate gradually and it may be a very difficult, deeply upsetting process, which other factors in the person resist. Their resistance often generates acute psychic storms as well as psychological problems. The process of detachment does not only occur in early childhood or adolescence. It may be experienced whenever a person has accepted a limiting, but perhaps much-needed structuring relationship giving a sense of order and security to the confused and anarchistic personality—whether it be a relationship to another person (as in marriage), or to a set of religious or socio-ethical assumptions which at the time appear relevant and valid. If the process of individualization is "successful" in the sense that it does not merely emphasize and make rigid an ego intent on forcefully and jealously asserting its independence from all situations, this process may lead to the next stage in the possibility of development of a human type of subjectivity. I have referred to that stage as the state of *individual selfhood*.

This state assumes the at least relative independence of the subject, "I," from existential situations, but its legitimate evolutionary development necessitates a new factor which may be slow to develop: a sense of responsibility for choices that now can be made freely as an independent as well as autonomous "individual person." The detachability of the subjective factor from human experiencing acquires a positive meaning only when the subject assumes responsibility for the selection of one of several alternatives. Only then can the process prove itself attuned to the essential quality of the cyclic tide of being during the long human period of the cycle—from the symbolic Noon to Sunset.

The next stage in the development of human subjectivity, the Pleroma type of subjectivity, can only be reached through a lengthy, arduous, and often tragic process of radical metamorphosis of the three factors implied in human experience. The desires of the relatively isolated subject have to be transmuted; the formative and structuring mind has to operate in terms of transpersonal, integrative and compassionate desires free from biological and cultural compulsions; and a new kind of energy has to be made available. It becomes available after the strictly biological type of organization has become transubstantiated, and eventually totally attuned to, a super-biological and planetary kind of power gradually being concentrated in the Pleroma.

The condition of subjectivity manifesting at the

Pleroma level evidently transcends our mental power of understanding. One can only state that a difficult-to-imagine combination of individual selfhood and group-unanimity seems to operate in it. Though it is a stage of the Movement of Wholeness beyond the strictly human state, Pleroma beings are still related to humanity and its evolution. They participate in that evolution at both an objective and subjective level—thus as controlling factors in the evolution of the planet, and as inspirers and guides for human individual selves struggling to overcome their attachment to both biology and culture. What the unfoldment—or rather the *in*foldment—of Pleroma consciousness means cannot be suggested, except that it seems logical to relate it at a certain stage to the radiant state of starhood instead of to the dense and heavy condition of planethood. This implies a galactic or cosmic situation. The process reaches its ultimate possibility of fulfillment in the Godhead state —a state of nearly absolute subjective oneness. In that state subjectivity operates as total, all-inclusive Compassion, the supreme and most sublime mode of desire. Through divine Compassion a new world is created, a new opportunity for the failures of the past to reach the fullest possible experience of Wholeness.

As the principle of Multiplicity asserts itself once more after the symbolic Midnight, the trend toward an objective actualization of the Godhead's compassionate desire in the concrete substantiality of an eventual state of planethood assumes an ever greater influence in the Movement of Wholeness. The almost totally unified Mind of the Godhead—the eonic Mind that experiences a whole cycle in a timeless instant—differentiates into "celestial Hierarchies," each of which represents a single basic aspect of the Godhead's Mind.

This mind—as we shall presently see—is *involving* through a series of transformations which the human consciousness can only intuitively perceive as reflected images. Esoteric traditions tell us that during this period of involution (from the symbolic Midnight to Sunrise) the two great principles of Unity and Multiplicity are in a state of what we may interpret as "conflict"—just as we think of conflicts when considering the often stressful, symmetrical relationship between the many egos and an organized society during the period of evolution of humanity (from Noon to Sunset). Various mythological narratives refer to "wars in heaven," and religious traditions give great importance to the personification of the process of division and differentiation gaining momentum during the rise of the principle of Multiplicity—a principle which always acts as a denial and repudiation of any experience of oneness.

Though in the situation religions assume to be the Creation of the universe the two great principles of Unity and Multiplicity are of equal strength, *the desire to be many* and to experience being in a multitude of ways has an aggressive kind of power. It forces the trend toward Unity to retreat (as it were) inward. All the latter trend can do is to contain the expansive energy of whorls of protomaterial and subatomic elements within spiral-like structures. What was once subjective *centrality* uses its available energy in order to build and give a firm reality to *circumferences*. Mind operates within these circumferences, impressing the existing archetypal structures upon the plastic and receptive substratum of being which not only fills space but (in its essential Beness) *is* space, the infinite ocean of potentiality.

Even at the primordial level of beingness called "matter" we should assume the existence of a subjective factor in the elements with which the human mind has to deal. Hydrogen, iron, or uranium "experience" at their level of wholeness; but obviously the nature and quality of these experiences and of the subjective factor in them differ vastly from those of human experiencing, because the situations being experienced in both instances differ so greatly. Yet the dualism of atomic or chemical attraction and repulsion, present in all matter, is analogous to what is experienced in human situations as a pleasure/pain, love/hate or success/failure polarization.

This dualism takes a somewhat different form at the level of biological organization, especially when a differentiating type of structural replication operates as sex. Mind then is feverish with the urge to discover new techniques of self-multiplication which makes possible the haunting satisfaction of the increasingly differentiated desires of an atomized kind of subjectivity. However, when the phase of maximum multiplicity is reached, a reversal of the cyclic Movement occurs. After this symbolic Noon, the strictly human type of subjectivity begins to be a possibility because new situations, now with a human character, result from the altered relationship between the principles of Unity and Multiplicity. As we shall see, these situations are profoundly affected by the mysterious but powerful Presence of the quasi-divine prototype of personhood, the Supreme Person.

The expenditure and repotentialization of energy

Energy, understood in its most fundamental nature, is the product of a dynamic state of relationship. The concept of Wholeness implies such a state, whose two polarities are the principles of Unity and Multiplicity. As these are polar opposites of equal strength, alternately and cyclically waxing and waning, the movement their relatedness produces is balanced. It is a state of dynamic equilibrium. The energy unceasingly generated by the harmonic process of bipolar relatedness is as constant as the structure of the cyclic relationship is invariant. In its most basic sense, the word *Space* (capitalized in order to avoid misunderstanding) refers to both the dynamic state of balanced relatedness and the energy inherent in it. Space is a plenum of energy because it is fullness of relationship.

Any relationship implies what normally is called space. If there is no space (no dis-stance) between two entities, they cannot be considered related, provided we do not limit the idea of distance by thinking of it in terms measurable by physical yardsticks or any other material means of measurement; thus, in terms of what can properly be called "di-mension."* But this dimensional and measurable space is not Space (capitalized) any more than personal emotions are cosmic Motion, or the love/hate dualism that so often tears the integrality of human persons is the changeless relationship between the principles of Unity and Multiplicity. This relationship generates energy, and energy inheres in Space in both the potential and kinetic modes.

Potential energy is expended as kinetic energy when the desire for its use arises in a subject confronted by a situation requiring the use of energy. The energy used does not vanish from Space; it becomes dis-organized. At least part of this energy ceases to be concentrated within the structure of a finite field of being in which a subjective factor is an active presence, able to manifest as a source of desires and perhaps of will. As this energy

---

*Two entities occupying the same area of space at the same time are not related; they constitute a single entity. The concept of knowledge through what is assumed to be "identification" is the result of a semantic confusion. Perfect *resonance* is meant, not identification. Similarly, a reflection is not the "real" source of the light-rays.

is used in various modes of activity, it becomes scattered and loses its cohesion. Yet it may also be repotentialized and once more condensed within a field
of being. The potential energy which had been kineticized and spent by the multitude of biological
species in a biosphere almost frantic with differentiation and proliferation is repotentialized when the trend
toward Unity asserts itself with sufficient power. However, this mainly occurs during the last phases of human
evolution, still far in the future for the masses of
humanity. It presumably is one of the functions of the
planetary Pleroma.

Today the type of expenditure of energy engendered
by sociocultural and interpersonal relationships can
already be controlled, neutralized, and repolarized as
part of a process of conscious and willful repotentialization. I have already mentioned such a process in terms
of a somewhat different frame of reference when speaking of asceticism, or the conservation of energy. This
demands either attunement to the rising trend toward
Unity, or an intense devotion to the Avatar who once
gave concrete form to a new archetype—the great
symbols and myths of the culture which developed
mainly after the dissolution of the Avatar's bodily field
of existence. Both approaches are valid, yet one of them
is usually the dominant factor in a person whose
dharma befits him or her for such a repotentializing
activity.

It should be clearly understood that energy is never
created. Energy is the substratum required to enable
any organized whole of being to experience Wholeness. But the quality and intensity of the experience is
basically determined by the level of beingness at which
this whole can operate. While the energy is always
"here," it may be too diffuse to be useable in the fulfillment of a conscious or subconscious purpose. Space is

a plenum of energy; yet the state of plenitude does not imply the possibility *effectively* to use what fills the space-field. There must also be condensation and concentration.

In science, space can be thought of as a dimensionless mathematical point, but this is a strictly formalistic meaning, and Western science is indeed a formalistic system of interpretation of data provided by physical senses.* In a deeper sense, Space can be condensed in a nearly unextensive area (or core of being), or it can be diffused in terms of quasi-infinite extension. Yet, according to the philosophy of Operative Wholeness, Space and the plenum of energy it symbolizes can never reach a state of infinite density and become an absolute center of Beness, "the One." Neither can Space be absolutely fragmented and differentiated in an infinity of "ones" unable to experience any desire for relationship because they are synchronously deprived of useable energy. To repeat a previous point, there can be no absolute states of either Unity or Multiplicity —only states of maximum oneness or multiplicity which, when reached in a cycle, call forth at once a reversal of the Motion and radically alter the character of the ever-changing but always cyclically balanced experience of relatedness.

Energy is usually defined as the capacity to perform work. As it performs work it operates in its kinetic mode; but before the performance mobilizes it, the energy is "present" in a potential state. It is mobilized or kineticized either by a natural change in a situation producing a basic need, or by some kind of intentional personal desire. As it passes from a potential to a kinetic state, energy seems to be "spent"; yet it is not lost. It

---

*See *Rhythm of Wholeness*, chapter twelve, p. 198, for a definition of science.

merely changes state and passes to a lower level of potentiality, especially becoming heat. If it were continually spent for the satisfaction of a multitude of needs or desires, the energy potential of any organized system of activity would sooner or later be dissipated. This dissipating trend is what is now called entropy, and it would lead to a "dead level" of energy. However, entropy applies only to closed systems of being. In open systems an opposite process, negentropy, is also at work.

This process manifests in a variety of ways. At the biological level we see it operating as eating and feeding (in the most general sense of the words). Through eating, the spent biological energy is restored; but restoration can only operate within relatively narrow limits, and the life-system that was born must die. It dies in a state of biological impotency. It must do so because the principle of Multiplicity aggressively dominates the realm of life-systems, and the principle of Unity can only maintain the operation of the system as a whole between two markers of time, birth and death.

At the sociocultural level, the process of negentropy assumes the character of "information." In childhood one may refer to it as the process of education; but what is usually called education is actually instruction. To be "in-structed" is to be fed informational data, operational formulae, and officially tested and validated techniques. At the level of the collective mind, the nature of such an intellectual "food" conditions the character and quality of the energy which the culture is using. Yet at the very core of the collective societal organism, a little-understood kind of energy is also operating. It has been developing and making itself felt through the simple fact of human togetherness and cooperation. It is the energy of *psychism*.

Psychism operates in terms of often rigid principles of organization, and through the binding power of great myths, symbols, and deeply rooted common feelings. It may be compared to the energy which keeps the activities of many types of cells functionally integrated and consistent; yet a basic difference exists between the life-force and the power of collective psychism. The former belongs to the *involutionary* arc of the cycle of being; the latter to the *evolutionary* process characterizing the development of humanity, a development which (at the symbolic Noon) follows the great reversal of the Movement of Wholeness and the manifestation of the Supreme Person in whom the Solution for the ancient karma is embodied. Yet at first the power of biological instincts is still so compelling that the energy of psychism is hardly distinguishable from the power of the life-force. Similarly, the subjectivity factor which, in the experiences of prehuman organisms, was centered in the whole species rather than in any particular specimen, remains identified with the entire tribe. It is often projected upon a superphysical realm assumed to be "spiritual" (though it is only psychic or "astral") as the god of the tribe.

This god is endowed with the attributes of personhood, but it is the kind of personhood which the collective mind of human beings, still so close to the biological level, is able to picture; and the picture is at first very crude. In it the balanced cyclic Motion of the Movement of Wholeness can only be experienced as "emotion," and the energy produced by the harmonic tension between the opposite and complementary principles of Unity and Multiplicity is interpreted as the Will of a personal god.

According to the religious approach to existence, the means to effect a degree of repotentialization of energy are identification with the divine will, total

devotion to the ideal of personhood spiritually manifested as a god, and a rigid control of the expenditure of
energy through simplification of interpersonal relationship and even asceticism. The process of neutralization
or absorption of ancient karmic failures does not demand an expenditure of energy; instead it implies a
repotentialization of energy. This process inevitably
acquires a stronger momentum when, at the symbolic
Sunset, the strength of the principle of Unity begins to
overcome that of the trend toward Multiplicity, which
by then is in retreat and in a defensive role. In the
Pleroma type of organization the process of repotentialization leads to an increasing condensation
of energy.

Space itself is being condensed. This condensation
process is the polar opposite of the cosmic scattering
and differentiation of energy which followed the
"Creation" of the universe, now given a new form
(perhaps as mythological!) as modern science's Big
Bang. The repotentialization of energy through a
hierarchical series of metacosmic and predominantly
subjective Pleroma states leads to an *almost* total concentration of energy and space. Space is condensed
into an increasingly small area, yet can never be reduced to a mathematical point. Moreover, all quantitative values and the possibility of measurement are
evidently not applicable to such a "divine" state. In this
Godhead state everything may seem possible, and
potential energy might be considered infinite. Yet as
immense Compassion arises, the Solution envisioned
has to balance and exactly fit the karmic remains of the
by then concluded cycle. Everything is possible that
is *needed*.

Energy is always there, available; but the character of
that available energy is determined by the balance
of power of the two principles of Unity and Multiplicity

in that particular phase of the Movement of Wholeness. The availability of the power is also related to the nature and material characteristics of the locality at which energy is to be used. What we call "matter" is a condition in which energy has reached a degree of stability. Matter (or in a more general sense, substance, whether or not it is "physical") is energy in form; and as we shall presently see, form (in the true sense of the word) is the basic product of the mind factor. However, this is mind operating at a cosmogenetic, biogenetic level and, during the human period of evolution, as builder of the complex structures of a vast series of cultures. Each culture is intended to stress a particular aspect of the supreme ideal of personhood which the Godhead had envisioned during the Midnight phase of the great cycle.

What is needed of the infinite potential of energy available to the Godhead at that Midnight moment of reversal of cyclic motion is used by the divine Mind, acting through what past mythologies have called "celestial Hierarchies" of Builders of the Cosmos. However, the mobilized energy is operating within the divine Mind, of which these Hierarchies are differentiated aspects. Each Hierarchy releases a specific type of energy which eventually, during the evolutionary development of humanity, will be characteristically available to a particular series of cultures. Human persons may become "agents" for the release of the energy or the basic archetypal structures that a Hierarchy, with which the persons are in tune, has created.

True "creativity" is the ability to reflect and concretize an archetype existing at the higher level of mind. Creativity should not mean merely or essentially personal "self-expression." If it does it has to be considered the release of internal tensions. Most of the time, however, it refers to the making of a product which answers the desire of a group of human beings, and may bring some kind of profit. But productivity should not be confused with creativity.

Internal psychological tensions do undoubtedly generate some kind of energy—but emotions operate at a level essentially different from that of cosmic or evolutionary movements.* These are attuned to what is intended and possible in terms of the karma-neutralizing process. They work *through* personhood, but they acquire the particular character and often inconsistent rhythm of emotional releases (perhaps interpreted as self-expression) engendered by the desires of a subject (I, myself) having separated itself from the cyclic process and intent on proving its freedom of choice. When this occurs, personhood becomes a means which insists on being an end in itself. This happens when mind provides a rationalized interpretation and justification for the desires of the subject of whom it has become a servant. That mind, however, may refer to a collective type of mentality superimposed upon the individual situation, whether this mentality is traditional and religion-based or the product of a generation's revolt against past standards. Mind can indeed be a tyrant after having begun as a servant.

Mind: intermediary, interpreter and technician

In any situation a desire is aroused. It may be an unconscious or a conscious desire; it may be the taken-for-granted motive that once led to the formation of a habit—a subjective manner of reacting to an often

---

*In my earliest work *Art as Release of Power* (1930) I stressed this distinction between Cyclic (or Cosmic) Motions and personal emotions, particularly in the chapter "Art of Gestures and Art of Patterns." A few copies of this essay are still available, though the whole book has long been out of print.

repeated situation. But however it manifests, and whatever the name given to it, the desire factor is operating, expressing a subjective state of being, a preference for a particular type of response.

The desire-motive requires the release of some kind of energy in order to be actualized; yet many psychologists and philosophers do not seem to realize that the subjective factor never deals *directly* with energy. A third factor, mind, is needed as an intermediary. Mind has to operate not only as a linking activity but as an interpreter and (in the broadest sense of the word) a technician.

In a famous illustration, the dualistic Sankhya School of philosophy in old India spoke of *purusha* (spirit) as being lame, and *prakriti* (the substratum of matter-energy) as being blind. Purusha is being carried over Prakriti's shoulder, showing the way to the blind. This is, however, an incomplete and misleading image; for while Prakriti may be blind, it is shown in the story to be organized as a body able and trained to walk, while the seeing Purusha can somehow choose (or is led to choose) one of several possible options in directing the steps (the operational activity) of Prakriti. A third activity is implied in the activities of the pair. This factor—mind operating at the biological level as a generic formative principle—has given an organically effective structure to the vital energies of the integrated collectivity of cells of the body; this body can at least walk. This same factor, operating at the level of culture and personhood, enables the desire to reach a goal (or at least to follow a definable direction) and to translate itself into a directive or order which can be transmitted to and sufficiently understood by the blind body of Prakriti.

Because the operations of mind are manifold and assume varied aspects, the whole range of the mind's

activity is not recognized for what it is. Yet these
activities should never be absolutely ignored or denied,
just as a subjective and a potency factor can never be
entirely absent from any situation. They may at most
be rendered temporarily ineffectual or intentionally
paralyzed in some special and abnormal experiences.
The inactivity of any one of the three factors may indeed be valuable in some special human situations, but
such an inactivity can only be a means to force an issue
which has produced intense stress and tensions. In the
best possible cases it may produce a state of extremely
focused "at-tention" to the possibility of solving a
problem posed by human free will; and free will is the
strictly human ability of the subjective factor to detach
itself from a situation and operate as an external and
assumedly unconditioned subject.

In one identifiable mode of activity or another, mind
operates in all situations, thus in all phases of the great
cycle of being. It is the operational aspect of the principle of Relatedness which is implied in the concept
and also the experience of Wholeness. It is a universal,
ever-present activity. It provides channels through
which the factors of desire and potency— one might also
say consciousness and power— may interpenetrate and
interact. These channels, however, can become too rigid
and control a process they are meant to assist and
indeed make effective. Starting as a servant, mind can
become a tyrant, blocking the expression of new subjective desires and keeping the will in a straight-jacket.
Mind indeed can so condition the acts of will that this
will becomes moulded by mental prejudices and idio-
syncrasies, especially by those which a collective
culture and family tradition have forced upon a child
since birth. Yet as we shall see, the restrictions and
restraints imposed by a culture have perhaps irreplace-
able value in allowing personhood to emerge with a

steady rhythm from the state of life. By limiting the possibility of options available to a child and adolescent, a cultural and religious tradition acts as a structuring factor providing a relatively calm and safe psychic, familial, and socio-political environment. When ideological or personal storms unfold their potential of violent mental transformation in the child's close environment, the development of an ego tends to assume a stressful and catabolic character, and personhood takes neurotic forms.

The main purpose of modern psychology, and especially psychotherapy, is to deal effectively with these forms. Philosophers compelled to become psychologists and analytical scientists by the spirit of the times (*zeitgeist*) try to reduce to mental processes the neurotic, experience-disorganizing tensions of the many persons seeking happiness and sociocultural fulfillment. Depth-psychologists dig into the subconscious of their clients in order to uncover the memories of unassimilated and rejected situations which impaired or distorted the flow of subjective desires and the capacity to mobilize will. Most psychologists and psychiatrists attempt to re-normalize the individual person and make him or her able to function more peacefully and productively in their society. But if they are successful, the result is likely to be the stabilization of personhood at the collective level at which the culture and its processes operate. It may be a stabilizing process, a strategic withdrawal needed to regain strength and re-establish an effective contact with the potency factor—what is realistically possible for the perhaps prematurely individualizing person in an unfavorable sociocultural situation. It may also be the unconsciously accepted loss of opportunity to raise the subjectivity factor to a new level and thereby to effectuate a transmutation of desire.

In all instances, mind is involved. Its activity is required as an intermediary between the subjective and potency factors. Mind has to interpret to the subject, eager to experience the fulfillment of desires, the ways of power—thus the effective modes of release of kinetic energy from a state of potential, non-operative being. Mind imagines solutions, invents instrumentalities and specific methods. Mind is the technician, concerned only with what can be reliably proven "to work" at the practical level of the control of natural energies. But mind also operates at another level in terms of the sequential emergence of phase after phase of the Movement of Wholeness. In fulfilling such a cosmogenetic function, mind is an impersonal or superpersonal evolutionary factor; while as it operates in the field of development of personhood, in most cases mind acts as a cogitative, discursive, argumentative and also conflict-producing factor responding to the pressure of conflicting desires as well as to the possibilities of using power for the satisfaction of these desires.

Because the cosmic scope of the universally operative first aspect of mind is only understood in a limited sense, and because so much confusion seems to exist in assessing the value and purpose of the function of mind in the development of personhood, the next chapter will be devoted to a study, brief as it must be, of these various levels of mental activity during the entire cycle of being.

6

The Formative and the Separative Operations of Mind

Mind and form

In its most fundamental aspect mind is the relatedness between the principles of Unity and Multiplicity as this relatedness operates throughout the cyclic process of the Movement of Wholeness. The character of the relation, Unity to Multiplicity, unceasingly varies, as one phase of the vast process of being follows another and announces the next. The nature of the activity of mind therefore also changes as the process unfolds and new situations arise. Nevertheless, the function of mind as revealer of the wholeness of any situation—and thus as an aspect of Wholeness—is essentially that of giving a *form* to the situation. Mind is always and everywhere the formative power of the beingness of any whole. In order to understand mind we have therefore clearly to realize what is implied in the concept of form.

As already stated, any whole is finite, since otherwise it should not be considered a whole; it is a system of organization of elements interacting within the boundaries of a "field," at whatever level of being this interaction occurs. Any finite field has boundaries which in some manner separate it from other fields, and these boundaries define its presence in terms of a particular shape and of the ability it may have to relate to and affect other fields. The enduring existence and activity of any whole also implies the internal operation of a principle of organization establishing more or less definite and permanent patterns of functional relationship between the many elements which constitute parts of this whole. These patterns, when understood in their operative totality, constitute the inner form (or structure) of the whole.

Unfortunately the words *form* and *shape* are often used interchangeably as exact synonyms, and this leads to a basic confusion found even in philosophical books, including books on Hinduism or theosophical doctrines in general.*

The shape of an object is an external factor which refers mainly to the actual or potential uses for which this object is intended—thus, the shape of a surgical instrument for an eye operation is determined by the structures of both an eye and the surgeon's hand. Generally speaking, the shape of an object is defined by the space and color relationship between an object and whatever surrounds it. Shape deals with external relations between a physically organized existential whole and other wholes, or between a well-defined

---

*The Sanskrit term *rupa* so important in Hindu metapsychology, has usually been translated as "form"; but I believe it refers to the concrete "vehicle" (*vahan*) necessary for the objective manifestation of a *quality* of being which can be evoked by sense perceptions and interpreted by the intellectual processes of the rational mind. It is claimed that these qualities can be experienced directly at a higher level as qualities without the need for a frame of reference which a *vahan* constitutes. Qualities, however, should not be considered formless. They are interrelated within the Godhead's vision of a new universe, as Letters are interrelated within the creative Word (the Greek "Logos").

system and the total environment in which it has to maintain its existence as a whole.

Form, on the other hand, refers to the specific state of relatedness of many elements contained in a field whose structural energies keep them integrated in terms of their function. The interpretation of the term *function* differs at every level of activity; for instance, the function of a melodic theme in a symphony differs in character from the function of the liver or adrenal glands in a human body. A discourse has form when the points the speaker makes follow one another in a consistent and ordered sequence revealing the workings of the principle of Unity in his or her mind. A work of art has form when every part of it concurs to convey a personal experience of Wholeness and meaning, or exemplifies a type of ordering and a traditional structure which pioneers in the development of the artist's culture had once envisioned as an archetype of relationship and institutionalized as a collective mode of expression.

Two different and indeed opposite types of formative processes have however to be distinguished. In one case, an area of space whose boundaries have been established is divided according to a cosmic or a biological principle of differentiation into regions intended to be the localities for the operation of specific functional activities. We see such a process operating when a fecundated human ovum divides into groups of cells which will become the organs of the fast-growing embryo. In another case, simple elements or wholes operating at a less inclusive level of integration come together, or are more or less forcibly brought together in order to constitute a more inclusive whole by accepting a schedule of organized and functional differentiations. This is the way in which a community of people, a business corporation, or a nation is usually formed.

In the first instance, the parceling of an area of space is involved according to geometrical principles studied in occult metaphysics, or according to genetic biological directives whose origin is unknown. In the second case, a building process occurs requiring the gathering of materials or people that may have belonged to some other system of organization, but have left or been wrenched from its field of integration. In both instances the result is a new whole of being which "has form," even if, at the level of an abstract system, one cannot really speak of its "shape."

The process of parceling of space refers, as we shall see, to the period during which the divine Mind, operating through celestial Hierarchies, gives form to the archetypes of the future universe envisioned at the symbolic Midnight by the Godhead's Compassion. Mind is then operating in its involutionary aspect. It becomes more specifically an evolutionary factor when, after the Noon (bottom) of the great cycle, its most essential task is the building of sociocultural institutions and religious systems and rites. Mind then increasingly attunes itself to the rising trend toward Unity, while during the earlier half of the cycle (from Midnight to Noon) mental processes were dominated by the principle of Multiplicity and the drive toward differentiation.

When they are stabilized, the forms which the involutionary mind evokes out of undifferentiated space, as well as those the evolutionary mind builds by the gathering and integration of scattered elements (physical or intellectual), have a common and essential characteristic: any form implies an inside and an outside. We can look at the distinction between inside and outside in terms of *shape* (the shape of an object or even of a discourse), or in terms of the internal principle of organization giving to the entity being considered its characteristic generic or individual structure—its *form*. But wherever mind works as a formative principle, the dualism of inside and outside cannot be totally dismissed as an unreal illusion. Shape, inasmuch as it refers to wholes of being, is the relatedness of inside and outside. However, such a relatedness acquires a different meaning at the Pleroma level, and the concept of shape is hardly valid in a predominantly subjective condition of being. Yet even a subjective state has an internal form; it excludes what the formative principle operating in it considers irrelevant or alien to the specific function of the whole. Thus a relative degree of exclusivity should be expected to exist even at the Pleroma level. The interpenetration of the consciousness of the beings integrated in a particular Pleroma organization does not preclude their common realization that they are components of a particular whole fulfilling a definite function in a still vaster Pleroma.

Such a function both includes and excludes other functions. In terms of a *consciousness* increasingly dominated by an all-encompassing subjective realization of Oneness, it presumably includes all other functions. But in terms of *activity* and of the power used in such an activity (however subjective and unexperienceable by human beings it may be), a degree of exclusivity has to be assumed. Every mode of power has its own rhythm and vibratory character, even though ideally they all combine into an immense Chord of being. In the Godhead state this Chord is almost one single Tone—but only almost. If there were no discordant vibration in that Chord—no memory of past failures which inevitably arouse Compassion in the Godhead— there could be no new universe, and therefore this present one would not have begun, and the writer of these words could not possibly exist.

While the internal form of a "lesser whole" determines

its function in a larger system of organization of many
other wholes, the function of each of them is interpreted
by the consciousness of the larger system as also constituting its meaning; and with the concept of meaning
the level of esthetical response is reached. *Ethical
judgment* is based on the exclusion of alternatives which
do not "con-form" to either an individual or a collective
judgment, value, truth, or even reality. *Esthetical
response*—at least when free from cultural prejudices
and personal memory-associations—includes all the
elements of an external situation in their interrelatedness.

In an esthetical response to a painting the interrelatedness of the colors and of the shapes they evoke
is the factor generating the realization of the meaning
of the painting. But if the viewer brings to the viewing
of the painting the feeling that the color red, whenever
stressed, is ugly and evidence of destrucive energy, his
or her reaction is ethically preconditioned. The pre-
conditioning may be intellectual or emotional; it may
be determined by the collective paradigms of the
culture or the result of personal memory-reactions. In
either instance the possibility of a truly esthetical
response to the whole organization and meaning of the
painting is at least partially destroyed. In the case of an
ink drawing or engraving, form results from the contrast between black lines or areas and the white background. To consider the black evil and the white good is
hardly possible, yet the shapes of the black lines or
areas may suggest (or indeed intend to depict) un-
pleasant previous experiences in the world of nature
or social activity; and as a result the ethical response
may be obscured by emotional reactions. All characteristically emotional reactions have indeed an implied ethical basis: "This is good or bad for me, for my
group or the society in which I participate."

When decisions have to be made in terms of a subsequent action which has to be performed or ordered, an either-or situation confronts the person who then has to operate as a subject charged with an executive choice. In some cases the choice obviously has to be made in terms of subjective desire with often immediate results: "I want what will happen, or I fear the consequences." In many other instances the issue is not emotionally charged; yet in all situations mind operates. It argues internally or in discussions with other minds, either on the basis of operative principles, group-traditions, and general social or business practices, or under strong personal feelings, intuitions, or even "voices" heard "inside the head." Such a level of mental activity implies that the subjective factor in the experience has become detached from the situation as a whole.*

The possibility for the subjective factor in an experience to detach itself from the experienced situation is, as I already stated, the characteristic feature of the human stage of evolution. Freedom of choice requires such a detachment. It requires facing human situations with at least a degree of objectivity; and mind provides what is needed for objective response: discrimination. Discrimination, however, implies analysis. Analysis requires a separation of the analyzing mind from what it analyzes, and it also necessitates some kind of fragmentation—the fragmentation of a whole into parts, which in turn can be studied objectively as wholes fragmentable into smaller parts, and this *ad infinitum.* This is the type of mental procedure followed in our

---

*Words here are confusing, and the evolution of Western philosophy has emphasized such a confusion by reversing the meaning of subject and object. A subject detached from its experiences becomes an object to other subjects who (or which) it regards as objective entities in another world.

present-day Euro-American science, and adopted by the greater part of mankind because "it works." The atom bomb worked! Where will mankind be led by such a mind whose stubborn association with ego gives an unquestioned validity and power of decision? This is a still unanswered and today unanswerable question.

The ego-mind is not the formative mind which operates in all phases of the Movement of Wholeness. It is only the first manifestation of a mind conditioned, and in a sense at least deviated and de-naturalized, by the development of the detachable type of subjectivity introduced in the earth's biosphere by our present-day humanity. It is the homo sapiens' mind. The image of such a mind's restless and argumentative activity should not obscure and distort the overall function of mind which is a cosmogenetic and form-building factor throughout the great cycle.

I shall now briefly suggest how this morphogenetic mind operates in the most characteristic phases of the cycle. But it is quite evident that when reference is made to prehuman and posthuman stages of being, only a *reflection* of situations which transcend the possibility of human experiencing can reach even the most sensitive intuition.

Mind as an omnipresent formative factor

It is logical to start such an overview with the symbolic Midnight phase, because the potentiality of a new universe then takes form in the Godhead, incited by supreme Compassion for the failures of the concluding cycle. The Godhead state constitutes the extreme degree of subjectivity and unification possible during a cycle; yet such a state of being is a "situation" just as any other particular balance of power between the principles of Unity and Multiplicity. The subjective factor is not the only one active in the Godhead's experience of this extreme Midnight situation, just as the principle of Unity does not *absolutely* overpower the principle of Multiplicity. The subjective factor in the Godhead situation is the most sublime expression of "desire": desire as all-inclusive Compassion. But this divinely subjective impulse can only be actualized in concrete and conscious experiences when the factor of potency is simultaneously mobilized. As already stated, the once "spent" energy of the previous universe has become repotentialized between the symbolic Sunset and Midnight phases of the cycle. Everything is possible in this Godhead state. Yet what the Godhead "envisions" is that set of possibilities which will produce just the required new opportunities for the failures of the past to neutralize their ancient karma under new cosmic and planetary conditions. The Godhead's vision impregnates, as it were, the Eternal Virgin that is Space itself—Space as the infinite Ocean of potentiality.

Impregnation implies not only two polarized factors, but a process linking them. This process is the activity of Mind in its most inclusive and unified divine state—the mind of wholeness in its supreme state. This mind is inherent in the Godhead experience of the symbolic Midnight of the cycle. It *gives form* to the divine desire for a new cosmos. But this form is still only an ideal formula of relationship connecting a multitude of possible answers to the ancient karma. The formula is an almost entirely subjective response to the divine desire. It develops gradually into a vast number of archetypes, through a process which involves the various aspects of the divine Mind—aspects which have been mythologized into "celestial Hierarchies." Each Hierarchy is said to project its own characteristic nature into the womb of Space.

A finite area is set apart or outlined as the future field

of cosmic activity. It is throbbing with processes of archetypal formulation. This activity takes place *before* the Creative Act marking the beginning not only of the universe but of the time which provides potential rhythmic patterns for the development of the world of energy-matter. Stirring this differentiating and formulating activity of the divine Mind is the gradual ascent to power of the principle of Multiplicity. The "sooner" (from our time-sense perspective) the Creative Act is to come, the more effective that principle, and the more differentiating the activities of the Hierarchy at work. The purpose of the entire process which antedates the world of physical matter is to define basic principles of organization which will operate as structural patterns within limited fields of forces. There must be an immense number of such patterns to answer the need imposed by the karma of past failures. And there must have been many ways for free human beings to introduce disharmonic surface variations in the tidal process of the Movement of Wholeness during the "Afternoon" period of the preceding cycle.

According to the Big Bang theory of modern astrophysics, the universe begins in a tremendous release of energy. Many religious Creation myths confirm such a single operation; yet other doctrines suggest several Creations, or rather a creative process occurring serially at several levels. Seen from the perspective of the Movement of Wholeness, there is one moment when the two opposite principles are exactly of the same strength but with the principle of Multiplicity in an aggressive kind of ascendency. This situation would seem to provide the theoretical basis for a single creative Act. But what is meant by "creation" may refer to the initial appearance of the most primordial and undifferentiated protomatter (perhaps a superphysical kind of hydrogen). Matter, according to this cosmological outlook, is energy stabilized by mind within a form. At the level of the equal relationship between the principles of Unity and Multiplicity above-mentioned, that form should be the most fundamental of all archetypal structures. It may be a kind of spiral formation, for a spiral-like type of motion is one in which the expansive power of the principle of Multiplicity has just become more powerful than the unifying principle of circularity.

The period extending from the symbolic Sunrise to Noon is marked, in terms of the development of the mind factor, by the involution of archetypes into the initial tumult of primordial energy-substance, feverish with the desire for differentiated and self-multiplying existence. Still strongly influenced by the principle of Unity, mind works to contain the explosive expansivity of the drive toward Multiplicity within archetypal structures. It is the servant of the inertial power of relatively stable cosmic, and later on biological formations. Biological processes may have their roots in interstellar galactic space, but their active manifestation requires conditions operative only in the state of material existence provided by dense and opaque planets—the state of planethood. Energy becomes stabilized into matter within a planet, and eventually the processes characteristic of "life" develop within material aggregations through a kind of functional specialization produced by the involution of archetypes of biological organization. Life-species become increasingly differentiated, but as a result their span of existence decreases. What they experience as time is the process of biological change bounded by the markers of time: birth and death. *Each species has its own time,* and the rhythm of its own life-processes.

The influence of the principle of Multiplicity increases

until the symbolic Noon when, having reached the possible maximum of power, it is challenged by the rising principle of Unity. Cyclic motion reverses itself. But before it does, the planet's biosphere has become the stage of a fever of self-differentiation and self-replication of which modern biologists and paleontologists have, I believe, no conception. Fossilized remains are only partial indications of conditions existing on long-submerged land masses; and prehuman races have gradually been built, approximating the structural patterns characterizing homo sapiens. The archetype, MAN-Anthropos, is gradually being impressed upon biologically operative substance. The process leads to the manifestation at the highest level of physicality (the two higher "etheric" sublevels) of the prototype MAN. I have referred to such a manifestation as the Supreme Person, inasmuch as I see in personhood the Solution envisioned by the Godhead in order to meet the need of the failures of the ancient past. It is such a Solution, however, only when through a long evolution it has reached a fully concrete and individualized state of operation which the Supreme Person had not only announced but catalyzed.

This situation—the state of personhood—implies the possibility of freedom of choice. Such a freedom is the result of the relationship which, after the symbolic Noon, develops between the rising principle of Unity and the still dominant but largely internalized and psychically effective principle of Multiplicity. Personhood develops, as we shall see, first at a collective level —because it is dominated by the inertia of biological (cellular and organic) processes—then in individualized ways. The desire for individual existence (*tanha* in Sanskrit) is centered in the human person, while at the level of life it has been (and remains) centered in the species. This manifestation of the principle of

Multiplicity in human persons operates both as new types of individualized desires and as new distinctive and singular ways of exteriorizing and actualizing these desires. These ways (or one might say "techniques") of fulfillment are presented by mind to the human "subject" eager for free decisions and experiences it considers "its own." However, through a long period of human evolution these are not in tune with the rhythm of the Movement of Wholeness. They create strife, confusion, and often tragedy. They engender karma.

These results refer to the level of mental activity which characterizes the ego-mind; but they still occur when the mind is on its way to a more integrated and conflict-free state of operation, yet still insecure and apt to be misled by or to overreact to complex internal situations. Besides this insecurely individualized mental activity, formative processes of a larger scope are at work at the beginning of any enduring and stable culture. They are brought to a focus in the initiating Avatar of the culture and released into the chaos of a disintegrating social order by a few of his disciples, acting as a germinating "seed."

The basic myths, rites, ethical principles of interpersonal and social relationship, and paradigms of the whole culture are products of the formative aspect of the mind; but this is *not* the ego-mind. It is mind as a formative principle and acting as a foundation for the development of personhood. Such a foundation is essentially archetypal, but as it manifests in a particular society, it is at first a collectively accepted pattern of thinking-behavior. From collective it becomes individualized through the process I have called "the process of individualization."

The Supreme Person is a perfectly individualized person. But it is a singularity, a single prototype, whose beingness at the symbolic Noon of the cycle can only operate at the sublevel of the physical realm where perfect integration is possible because it reflects the Godhead state of almost total oneness. The singleness of the Supreme Person therefore has to become the "multi-unity" of the Pleroma state, consummation of human evolution at the symbolic Sunset phase. I speak of multi-unity, because in that phase the principles of Unity and Multiplicity are of equal strength. A Pleroma is constituted by a multiplicity of individualized selves that nevertheless are a "Communion" of co-conscious beings. In that situation, planetary in scope, the operative mind is the fully developed mind of wholeness.

The mind of wholeness is the mind that *consciously and freely* accepts the karmic solution to the problems once caused by at least partial failure. All life-situations have to be accepted in the fullness of their implications, however dramatic the results may be. The transmutation of basic desires has to be achieved, but mind is always needed as the technician. Perhaps the technique has been learned "before"—in some old manifestation of personhood directly related to the present attempt. But the way to use the potential energy of one's nature (physical as well as psychic) in any case has to be mentally determined anew in each life-span. This way may be determined by the traditional models and procedures of the culture; it may also result from an involuntary and previously uncharted type of investigation, struggle and discovery.

What mind actually is, as a formative power in the Pleroma state that leads to the Godhead, cannot be directly known by a human person because the condition of personhood and its principles of organization have first to be transcended. I have already spoken of the process of repotentialization of energy and the condensation of Space. It seems that the complexities of the mind operative in personhood, and therefore at the stage of culture and social interrelatedness, have to be gradually reduced to a state of simplicity—irrespective of what Teilhard de Chardin may have believed. But this process of condensation does not mean a decrease in intensity. It implies an increase in speed of motion—a heating up process. Yet what we experience and interpret as heat may be a poor approximation of the character of the Pleroma state which is primarily a subjective condition of being, and has very little to do with molecular motion or even subatomic activity.

The Pleroma state cannot be totally subjective. Individuality and unanimity somehow must be integrated in a system of organization that transcends not only the human condition but the planetary level of reality. In such a system, revealing itself in the radiance of its component units, radiance does not mean expenditure of energy, but rather an ever greater condensation of potential energy. In the Godhead state marking the consummation of the one-ward period of the cycle of being, Space and potency are almost totally concentrated in what, to the human mind obsessed with and confused by multiplicity, must appear to be one Being. Yet it can only be *almost one* Being, for absolute Unity is inconceivable. There is always and everywhere Multiplicity—even if it be only the memory of the many failures with which the "almost One" had been associated in the past universe. In the Godhead state, resurgent memory is transformed into Compassion; and the all-encompassing Mind answers the call for new forms of relatedness from the all-compassionate Godhead. The cycle continues, invariant in structure, yet never the same in the sequence of events, because the principle of Multiplicity always demands the possibility of differentiation.

Stated in such terms, the picture of the cyclic movement of being may seem so vast and unexperienceable
as to have little value for helping a distraught person,
confused by a variety of religious, metaphysical, and
sociocultural claims, to find emotional stability and
inner security. Yet such a picture can be a guiding
dynamic structure in all basic situations which an individualized human consciousness has to meet. However, it should be understood to be an abstract formula
whose effectiveness does not depend on the level of
reality and feeling-experience at which the individual
operates at any particular time, as long as he or she
operates as a whole.

The Godhead state is present at the human level of
personhood to the extent that its presence is possible.
It is implied in the subjectivity of the deepest dreamless
sleep—a situation in the life of every human being.
Similarly, the Supreme Person could be a daily revelation of the power of personhood as one awakens at the
dawn of a new day. All the periodically experienced
phases of daily and seasonal existence can indeed be
given cosmic and metacosmic meanings without losing
any degree of practical efficacy and validity. The attribution of such cyclic meanings to every event and situation is implied in the ideal of living *sub specie eternitatis*.
This is symbolic living—existence experienced in terms
of essential and impersonal meanings. It is living not
only in the serene and inclusive acceptance of the
process of karmic readjustment, but also with a profound and unceasing *gratitude* for the compassionate
activity of those Beings who silently and unobservedly
perform, as much as the ineluctable rhythm of cycles
makes possible, the readjustment of anarchistic and
separative ego-activity to the tidal motion of the cycle
of being.

The discursive and argumentative mind

When a living organism, operating strictly at the level of biological organization, reacts to a situation, its reactions are determined by instinctual patterns characterizing the entire species to which it belongs. In computer terms, the organism is programmed to react in a specific way. Generally speaking, this way is the best which the desire for survival, self-replication, and expansion inherent in the stage of organization called life has yet found to fulfill itself in terms of what is possible for that particular biological species. The organism cannot choose another type of response. Whatever programmed the instinctual reactions left no other available option. From the point of view of the philosophy of operative Wholeness, the programmer is mind—mind operating as the formative power of biological evolution by impressing upon the sensitive material available in the biosphere definite structural patterns of action and reaction embodying archetypal formulas of relationship between cells and organs.

When, however, the great reversal of the cyclic motion of being occurs at the symbolic Noon, and a new balance of power between the principles of Unity and Multiplicity begins to operate, the new situation introduces a radically different type of possibility: the possibility of multiple options and of *personal choice*. The human person may use his or her will in an at least relatively or partially free manner. But this simply means that the person is able to bring to the experience of a new situation a subjective factor—a "desire" for or against—which is not determined by either a biologically set program of instinctual reactions, or a family, religious, and sociocultural tradition. Actually, however, any human person is first a living organism belonging to the genus homo sapiens, then a member of a particular family, class, culture, and social organization. The human being is therefore *at first* partially but inevitably programmed by the generic mind of his or her race and biopsychic ancestry, and by the collective mind of his or her culture. Yet being human, this person is able to disregard or oppose to some extent the instinctual reactions of his or her biological nature, and/or the imperatives of family and class traditions stamped since birth upon the interconnecting patterns of neuro-cerebral activity. The person can make choices on a personal basis as a singularity of being. He or she can choose to act in terms of what he or she desires (or fears) to experience.

Choosing to act, however, implies the selection or the working out of a succession of more or less clearly defined acts or processes. The subjectivity factor—the newly emerging desire or the sharply focused and concretizing will—may be present; but there is a gap between a desire and the concrete acts involved in its fulfillment. Only mind can bridge this gap. At the biological level of organization, mind does the bridging according to the archetypal patterns produced by the celestial Hierarchies. The mental processes are not free even though mind may *seem* to act by directly, spontaneously, and randomly reacting to the nature of the energies operating in the biosphere. But when the development of personhood begins and the subjectivity factor in human experience is able to detach itself ever so slightly from the situation a human being has to meet—only then can mind operate in relation to subjective desires having a "personal" character. The desires are "personal" in the sense that they are not totally determined by specific archetypal and/or cultural patterns. The essential character of personhood is revealed in the immense multiplicity of possibilities it encompasses. It must encompass them all because it is the "Solution" the Godhead envisioned for an equally great variety of ancient failures and therefore of karmic patterns to be neutralized.

It would be impossible, however, to pass at once from the state of totally compulsive biological organization to that of inherently free, autonomous, and responsible individual selfhood. It is equally impossible for the archetypally directed biological and generic mind to be transformed in one step into the mind of a totally individualized person. An intermediary phase of human evolution has been (and remains) necessary: the stage of culture. From the foundations of generic biological organization a *collective* type of sociocultural organization has had to emerge. It has been made possible primarily by the development of language and of other systems of symbolic intracultural communication, thanks to the development of the forebrain and of an immense number of neuro-cerebral interconnections. This "new brain" contains billions of cells which, though interrelated into many thousands of operative groups, seem to have a relative individuality of their own. In their totality these cells may be considered the many aspects of an all-human potentiality of personhood; thus they constitute or make possible the entire solution to the problem of karma envisioned by the Godhead. Though this solution is *potentially* operative at the highest levels of earth-matter in the prototype of personhood, the Supreme Person, it has to work out at the more material levels of existence where the karma of past "failures of nerve" or misdeeds have to be met consciously, without evasion, yet without engendering new disharmonic reactions.

Today, all but a relatively few human beings operate at the level of existence categorized as "personal." Yet this qualificative is ambiguous because the development of personhood has to pass through several phases; and in a forthcoming chapter I shall speak of several fundamental types of crises leading from one phase to the next. Each phase can be characterized by a specific type (or level) of subjective desire; and each of these desires calls upon the mind factor to provide a technique of operation assuring its satisfaction.

The ego-mind, in its primitive and crude forms, is the attempt by a newborn and growing child to find the most satisfying and pleasure-producing method of adapting its particular biological needs and relatively unique temperament to the pressures and demands of the familial and sociocultural environment. A particular strategy has to be devised—flexible or rigid as the case may be—in order for the child and adolescent to define his or her stand (and probably as a result, his or her status) within the biological family-group, the peer-group at school, and the social class of people to which the youth soon realizes he or she belongs. Mind is the strategist—but mind subservient to a desire-factor having become aware of its potential ability to partially control daily situations.

One can only control that from which one has to some extent become detached. In terms of the subjectivity factor (desire) one can speak of *detachment*, because it seems that an enfolding matrix-like structure to which one was attached is letting go, unable to resist the challenge of a new type of emergent energy. In terms of the mind's activity, subjective detachment becomes *separation*. This state of separation is objectively perceived and assessed as an incontrovertible fact in a new kind of situation.

Chaos (that is, the total lack of activity of the formative, order-producing power of mind) would be produced by a sudden, radical, and complete separation from the level of mental activity until then dominated by the archetypal power of instinct. This condition of chaos is avoided because a new type of organization (embodied in its prototype, the Supreme Person) enters the planetary stage. Moreover, the shift from the long-dominating principle of biological organization, "life," to the new principle, personhood, occurs very slowly. It occurs through gradual development of a long series of cultures whose collective patterns of order act as overtones of the fundamental tone sounded by biological processes. As these culture-building overtones are forms of organization less compulsive than biological drives, their power can be more easily challenged and overcome. What overcomes these drives is still the personhood principle of organization, but personhood in its individualized aspect: the individualized person operating, making choices, acting, and responding to other persons, *thus dealing with karma as a singularity of being.* Only where this state of individualization is achieved (which is *not* what Jung meant by "individuation") is personhood truly operative.

Personhood, however, can operate negatively—thus against the neutralization of karma—as well as positively. The ancient failure which produced the resurgence of karmic memory-patterns (subconscious though that memory is) may be repeated, and the patterns made less easily erasable; or ancient hate may be wiped out by Compassion. To repeat, personhood is what the Godhead envisioned as the Solution to the problems left by ancient failures; but whatever has to apply this Solution *has to be free not to do so* . . . and thus free to fail once more. It is a test of strength—thus, of the quality of the desire factor as it operates in a situation difficult to meet. It is also a test of the clarity of the mind. A clear mind—in the spiritual Buddhistic sense of the term "clear"—is a mind able to overcome the inertial power of the habits developed when the person was mainly controlled by the patterns of his or her culture, and also by the still more basic impulses derived from biological functioning.

Mind indeed finds itself in a difficult and precarious situation as the evolution, and especially the individualization of personhood proceeds, for it has to deal with conflicting forces. It has to deal with still very strong biological compulsions (hunger, sex, desire for self-multiplication and expansion of territory) and also with sociocultural imperatives impressed since birth upon the nervous system, brain cells, muscles, and metabolic functions. As participant in the collective activity and the psychism of a culture, the mind factor in the experience of personhood may have to fight against biological urges when cultural taboos or ascetic religious ideals are still powerful factors in a quasi-tribal environment. In any case, mind has to use symbols, words, and gestures belonging to the particular culture (or today the generational subculture) which had deeply influenced or controlled its growth, intellectual habits, and emotional responses or expectations. Mind has to deal with the karma of other persons with whom it is intimately related through life's shared purposes and activities, as well as with the personal karma of the ancient past.

The situation is indeed highly confusing because it repeatedly presents a variety of options whose validity can hardly be rationally determined. Though there is a deeply felt urge to take free and individual decisions, the decisions taken are not really free because they constitute the convergences of many event-lines whose origins and developments cannot be known by the mind of a normal person. What seems to be the relatively unimportant choice of a person moved unexpectedly by the rise of a strong desire may spark an unexpectedly wider series of repercussions. In any "personal" choice, much more may be at stake than the mind of a person advancing on the way of individualization or on the subsequent Path of discipleship; nevertheless, mental processes are always operating in any human situation. They operate in and through the immensely complex interconnection of cellular processes, chemical-molecular transformations, and electromagnetic currents, often conflicting with one another.

Because of such a situation, mind has very often been considered the enemy of spiritual development and the "slayer of the real." Mind has been compared to a noisy group of restless, chattering monkeys; and yoga has been developed to "control the operations of the mind." The usually unasked question, however, is: what could control these inconsistent random motions of a mind wandering from word to word, image to image, concept to concept, method to method, and even at times seemingly from purpose to purpose?

A traditional European psychologist-philosopher may answer: the will. But as will is a power, there must be a source to that power—some kind of being using it, directing it along some kind of path. From the Christian point of view, this source of will is the God-created Soul. The authors of the Upanishads presumably thought of it as *atman*. From the point of view of the philosophy of operative Wholeness the will, in its totally impersonal holontological aspect, is the Movement of Wholeness itself. It is the power that, in the cycle of being, drives one type of situation to the next. It is what the Zen master, asked to define Zen, may have meant when he said: "Walk on." But when the level of individualized personhood is reached, a subject, having detached himself from the cyclic Movement, assumes that he does the moving and the walking because he feels free to choose the direction of the walking. The choice, however, is determined by the desire to walk either with or against the tidal movement of evolution. And at a stage of evolution (in the symbolic mid-Afternoon), the trend toward Unity is becoming increasingly powerful, though not as yet dominant.

The subject, however, having detached himself from the Movement, may be unaware of and unconcerned by the direction of the motion. He may be too busy proving to himself and to others his independence from the culture that formed his mind, or even (as an adept proud of his abnormal powers) in perfect control of his biological and psychic energies. In the experiences of such an individualized person, the mind factor becomes a battlefield in which various desires are contending for mastery of the mental processes: the desire for a more abundant physical and emotional life, with greater happiness and/or comfort; the desire for wealth, social prestige, fame, power; the desire either to be more original and unique as an individual, or (out of sheer weariness and confusion) to renounce individual choice in order to find tranquility and what seems to be security by conforming to an ancestral tradition or a new mass-movement. Yet beyond these desires, the mysterious pull of a state of being transcending this "human, all too human" situation may also be recognized by a mind having been impressed in quieter moments by books or associates presenting this transcendent state not only as an ideal or utopia, but as an actualizable possibility of existence. In the midst of this conflict of desires, the karmic pattern of some ancient failure that once had occurred at a similar or related phase of the cycle of personhood (or a subcycle thereof) may operate. It may manifest as the resurgence of some unfinished situation seeking fulfillment, or as a sense of futility and depression, or in a variety of either clearly related or (more often) seemingly unrelated events. Mind has to deal with all of these factors.

Though it is the theoretical servant of the subjective factor seeking concrete fulfillment through the effective use of available energy, mind may cling to some old formula of its culture or religion, as to a plank of salvation. This may even further confuse the situation on the battlefield where desires are fighting against one another for the strategic use of the available power of the mobilized will. Moreover, once the subjective factor in the experience is detached from the evolutionary Movement, the now isolated subject finds itself dependent upon the forms and procedural techniques of the mind. When the person is operating at the ego level, trying to pass from compelling biological urges to sociocultural desires, the situation may not be too confusing for the mind; options tend to be limited by a for-or-against, either-or dilemma. But when the traditional patterns and the future development of the culture are sharply criticized by the mind in the *impersonal* terms of their validity as principles of organization, and at the same time are no longer able to satisfy the *personal* desires of the experiencing subject, the whole person may be involved in a difficult cathartic process of readjustment. Taking a resolute new step leading to a new phase in the development of personhood may require either a situation-altering external event, or a clearly focused and undismissible feeling-awareness of the reality of a transhuman stage of development just ahead.

Such a realization may be impressed upon the mind

in various ways, but it implies the directed activity of a factor operating at the culture-transcending Pleroma level. This factor is likely to be a particular Pleroma being to whose field of superpersonal planetary activity the individual in crisis potentially belongs. Such a being helps the struggling individual to realize the essential *place and function* which the individualized subjective self potentially occupies in the Pleroma. The so often mentioned Higher Self *is* that place and function. It refers to a spiritual Quality which is one of the many components of the "Soul" of the Earth-being—or, symbolically speaking, one among the myriad of Letters of the divine Word (Logos).*

As a truly individualized self, the subjective factor in personhood is only a single Letter, which in itself does not reveal the meaning of the Word (the creative Logos), yet which is indispensible to the fullness of that meaning. Such a Word, with its billions of Letters, constitutes the archetypal Solution envisioned by the Godhead in the Midnight phase of the Movement of Wholeness. Every fully individualized person is potentially one of these Letters. But one can significantly speak of "letter" only when one is aware of the "word" of which the letters are component parts. Similarly, an individualized person realistically points to and actually participates in the divine Solution, personhood, only when integrated with all other such persons.

A human society and culture are preliminary and transitional attempts to produce enduring structures of interorganismic and interpersonal integration; but these structures are still dominated by biological forces and rhythms. The Pleroma type of integration is based

---

*See *The Planetarization of Consciousness*, pp. 127-28.

on the use of energies that basically transcend the biological level of operation. It is based on the kind of individual selfhood which does not depend for its operation on what is perceived today as a physical body. The full power and meaning of personhood, as a totally effective Solution to the karmic situation having taken form as our planet Earth and all it includes, are actualized and understood only in terms of the Pleroma experience in which *all* individualized persons are to participate. This italicized "all," however, refers to what will be left of humanity in the omega phase of our cycle of planetary evolution (and in the larger sense, of the cycle of our entire universe)—the biblical "remnants," the Seed-Manu as a "race of Buddhas and Christs" (*The Secret Doctrine*, volume two, p. 483, original edition).

This Pleroma experience includes and requires the activity of a mind that has become at least aware of the operation of a superindividual (or rather trans-individual) principle of organization which is not limited to the level of cultural or social integration, but operates in terms of the whole planet. This new mind is the mind of wholeness to which I have referred several times. But it is also mind as the still unsure but dedicated servant of the subjective desire to identify one's personhood (if it has acquired an individualized form, distinct from the mass vibrations of present-day mankind) with the place-and-function in the planetary structure of the Pleroma which constitutes the person's supreme identity. This place and function are, as it were, waiting to be actualized; but the process of actualization requires the operation of a principle of organization which transcends the level of any culture and of a culturally defined personality whose name symbolizes its bondage to the psychism of the culture as a whole.

In the immense majority of instances today, the type of personhood actualized in molecular, biological, and sociocultural structures is only a crude approximation of what personhood means when understood in terms of the entire cycle of the Movement of Wholeness. Similarly, the ego-mind, or even the mind of an autonomous and responsible self, represents only a transitional state of mental development. It is a state still heavily dominated not only by the compulsiveness of life-instincts and the exclusiveness manifest in *any* culture, but by the pressures of karmic patterns. It is mind in crisis, trying to operate on the battlefield of warring desires, but pulled in rapidly altering directions by the ups and downs of the encounter.

The formalistic and inertial character of mental processes, and especially of their neuro-cerebral means of operation in biological and social terms, adds to the confusion. The unfamiliar and novel nature of the potency factor in such situations (that is, the nature of *social* power, manifesting today mainly as the possession of money) presents another set of problems.

The three factors in the type of experiencing possible at this new human level are involved in the difficulties and crises engendered by the development of personhood. The most basic problems in this "human condition" are derived from the capacity of the subjective factor to detach itself from a situation and to assume as an external entity the role of a subject, "I myself." In that role the subjective factor may have desires and preferences which do not conform to the developing trend and the rhythm of the Movement of Wholeness. Aroused by such disharmonic desires, mind also begins to operate in a state of non-resonance to archetypes which the divine mind had developed as Solutions to problems raised by the ancient failures. A "personal" mind replaces to a large extent the "archetypal" mind.

But today, as mentioned already, the term "personal" does *not* usually refer to the personhood manifesting in the Supreme Person as a divine solution to karma, but instead to a very limited and relatively individualized aggregate of desires. These desires, in most cases, remain dominated by biological needs and/or by a more or less violent reaction to the collective patterns of the basic culture and the popularized procedures and fashions of a class or a generation of human beings reacting to the emergence of a new kind of power. This personal mind, more or less a faithful servant of the desires of the individualizing subject, is adept at rationalizing and evading basic issues in the development of personhood. It should rarely be trusted as a constructive factor in complex crisis situations.

Mind can also act in such situations as a power of disintegration. The analytical mind, which fragments, reduces to what seems to it basic facts, and endlessly argues to prove its points, is a catabolic factor in the process of individualization. It can be very effective in breaking down old unsubstantiated beliefs and sclerotic patterns of thinking, feeling, and behavior. It may also disclose the massive, relentless, yet hidden operations of a will which (like a national Army and its leaders) has learned to use power for its own glory. Power may be used simply to perpetuate itself as a dominant force, either in a nation, or in an individual person racked by a poignant sense of insecurity and/or impotency. In such cases the danger to avoid is the growth of a super-ego (or super-individualized self) that becomes so separative and power-intoxicated that the development of a Pleroma type of integration is rendered impossible.

An answer to, or antidote for such a danger is provided by the rise of an intense feeling of devotion (*bhakti*) to a personage able to radiate at least some of the characteristic qualities of the Pleroma level of being. It should be, however, devotion to a *personage* as the performer of a role which should focus upon him or her at least a reflection of Pleroma power, rather than to a *person*. When such a devotion is a dominant factor, mental processes are usually devaluated. The ultimate purpose (consciously understood or not) is the transmutation of desire; yet the overcoming of the fear of being separated from the mass-vibration of the community at its normal level of operation, and thus of being isolated and alienated, may be the first requirement to be met. The *higher* Community (the Pleroma) always seeks to act, to help the individual subject in crisis. Nevertheless, karmic patterns may present obstacles which have to be dissolved; and the process of dissolution often operates in "strange and wondrous" ways.

A fundamental reorganization of the mind should be synchronous with a repolarization of the subjectivity factor. When the subject, I-myself, ceases to feel separate from the tidal flow of the Movement of Wholeness—thus, when personhood is reintegrated in the Movement and is conscious of itself as an essential polarization of the principles of Unity and Multiplicity —mind sooner or later is re-attuned to the process that created archetypes *before* the beginning of this objective material universe. In that attunement mind finds a strength that transcends the vagaries of the many systems of cultural, religious, and interpersonal relatedness. This strength is based on the realization of invariant principles operating through all cycles, long or brief as they may be. It is the strength of a consciousness free at last from the tension and the pride of individualized selfhood, and able to interpret and evaluate any situation *sub specie eternitatis*.

7

A New Frame of Reference: The Earth-being and the Function of Humanity within It

The development of frames of reference

If the character and quality of a specific type of knowledge and the expectable results of its application are being discussed, the most fundamental factor to be considered is the frame of reference used in the organization of the data this knowledge correlates. Knowledge implies data interrelated according to a few basic principles which the collective mind of humanity or a group or class of human beings accepts. These principles serve to define the place, the relative importance, and the meaning of the data within a frame of reference which is not only organizational but selective, inasmuch as it eliminates and excludes data which do not "belong," just as it provides patterns of integration for those that do.

Funk and Wagnall's Dictionary defines "frame of reference" as "the principles, circumstances, facts, values, etc., needed to inform or orient a person when thinking about, judging or interpreting something." In other words, a frame of reference establishes the basis on which a human mind operates when it attempts to deal with a situation in terms of data, principles, etc. which it considers true and reliable. Knowledge is not provided by the mere succession or simultaneous occurrence of unrelated events. It presupposes a principle of organization according to which the events or data or information have a specific place, and in many instances a function definable in terms of "law." This law is not only related to the frame of reference constituting the background of cosmic, natural, psycho-spiritual, or sociocultural order on which the law operates. Its usefulness and the value of its application are determined by the validity of the selective character of the frame of reference.

In the approach to everyday realities often spoken of as "commonsense," human beings deal with the information provided by the senses of their biological organism as it reacts to various kinds and levels of vibratory energy. These impacts reach numerous brain-centers where they become sensations. Persistent groups of sensations are interpreted by various mental processes as material entities, organic or inorganic, moving in an outer world. By entitizing repetitive groups of sensations into bodies it is possible for a person to operate more or less safely or successfully at either the biological or sociocultural level of actions and reactions. The more human beings "know" about the behavior and probable reactions of these entities, the greater their feelings of security, comfort, and presumably happiness, and also the greater their pride at seemingly being able to "control" the energies generated by motion—particularly through heat, gravity, or atomic disruption.

In the process of gaining the kind of control known as technology (and in a broader, more ambiguous sense, civilization), our Western world during the last centuries has used a specific frame of reference for knowledge: modern science and the scientific method. This has proven amazingly effective in organizing the results of an immense variety of data of observation. Nevertheless, this method, at least in the way it has operated since the seventeenth century, is highly selective. It excludes all information which does not conform to certain principles of acceptance and even to undemonstrable assumptions. Data for the development of the kind of knowledge approved by our official elite of university professors and scientists have to be obtained exclusively through the senses of the material human body, or through instruments extending the field of operation of these senses, according to rigorously defined procedures requiring a high degree of professional and academic specialization guaranteed by the State. Moreover, these data are considered useable at any time and everywhere in space. They are believed to provide a totally reliable basis on which "laws" and "constants" can be formulated. These mathematical formulations are abstractions which are then managed and correlated through intellectual processes which, in their togetherness, constitute "reason." Reason, at least as understood and used by the classical Greek and European cultures, is a principle of organization assumed to be strictly human and so superior as to be considered by many people as "God given," and greater than any other mode of mental activity. The language of higher mathematics is the rigorously precise by-product of the frame of reference established by the rationalistic mind under the name of logic. This frame of reference is exclusivistic insofar as it considers valid only what has reached the human consciousness, directly or indirectly through the physical senses, and can be interpreted in terms of the activity—*the measurable motion*—of material entities.

The rationalistic and scientific frame of reference

used by Western science may be traced back to Aristotle and some of his predecessors, but it only began to dominate European civilization after the Renaissance and the spread of Francis Bacon's ideas. It certainly was not the primordial type of organization of knowledge that developed in tribal cultures operating at the level of almost entirely biological considerations. Nevertheless, the use of the scientific method may be claimed to mark the beginning of mental maturity after a period of naive, childlike assumptions. One may also believe that mental maturity implies the superseding of a subjective type of interpretation of reality by an objective approach to existential data; yet this may be an only partially correct assumption. This kind of objectivity may represent the first stage of maturity—a reaction against the earlier (and not yet entirely vanished) condition of knowledge. This often violent reaction may inevitably produce very dangerous end-results. Because mankind has now to deal with them, it finds itself in a state of global crisis. In order to avoid a *planetary* disaster—and not only the collapse of all human values or even actual existence—a new frame of reference has not only to be formulated intellectually, but consciously and meaningfully *lived*. This frame of reference should be planetary, but the adjective *planetary* now has to be given a new and widely encompassing meaning. I have used the term "Earth-being" in order to suggest some of the implications of that meaning, which are still very difficult for even "New Age" persons to understand, and especially to accept as guiding factors in their lives.

A: Biocultural frames of reference

The development of a new type of organism—homo sapiens—in which new desires and a new mind were slowly taking form started from the strictly biological foundation of instinctual responses to vitalistic needs. The satisfaction of these needs was the one fundamental concern of whatever type of group-organization human beings established. As the specifically human capacity to communicate and to transmit the results of biological experiences to successive generations came to take enduring forms, these forms became the foundation of a particular culture. It was a particular type of foundation utterly conditioned by the character of the collective experiences the early tribesmen had in a strictly local ecosystem. These experiences were related to the seasonal processes of vegetation and the actions of animals capable not only of aggression but also of providing the food needed for survival.

A culture establishes a frame of reference for the experiences of a group of people intent on developing a more secure and pleasant way of surviving in an often inimical environment. This frame of reference enables the members of the culture to deal in as satisfying a way as possible with a more or less expectable series of recurrent changes and external events, the possibility being related to and limited by the "human condition" as this condition is experienced and understood at any particular level of human evolution. Whenever this evolution occurred from an animal state without any helpful and instructive contact with the remnants of a slowly-disappearing earlier and fully developed humanity, the earliest cultural frame of reference to be established by a human tribe constituted the attempt to define some kind of stable and effective relations, not only with animals and plants, but with rather mysterious transcendent entities assumed—and in some cases, actually perceived—to be responsible for either helpful or disastrous environmental changes. Such a frame of reference has been referred to as *animism*.

Animism is a system of organization enabling a community of human beings to meet in a relatively effective manner with daily and yearly recurring events identified as the actions of recognizable entities to which names could be given. A human person is also an entity having a definable character and a particular amount of usable energy. This energy is basically biological, but when belonging to a well-developed culture, a person is able to *control* events and processes of change through the development of the technical mind. At the animistic stage of mental understanding, and in terms of the knowledge which animistic cults and ways of life transmit and gradually make more effective, control operates on the basis of force against force. A biologically inferior force, however, may develop mental strategies (such as cunning, deception, sacrifice, and prayer) which can be expected to produce tangible results in relation to a superior force, especially if the latter is assumed to have an inherently beneficent character or to gain some kind of advantage from the operation.

In the terminology of modern philosophy—particularly the philosophy of science—atomism is taking the place of animism. The vibratory types of energy to which material atoms and particles have been reduced are not essentially different from the "spirits" with which shamans and ancient seers have dealt. However, while the concepts and practices of primitive animism had a strictly biological and ecological basis, modern scientific atomism assumes the objective existence of a non-living substratum called "matter." As we shall presently see, the possibility of measuring and dividing this matter leads to the development of a new and radically different frame of reference.

Spirits are identifiable entities to the extent that they act in a characteristic manner. A great multiplicity of spirits were believed to act in the life-environment of human beings, each spirit producing experienceable changes according to its specific quality and the form it would take while releasing its energy. However, when the approach to the collective experience of human beings took the form often known as *vitalism*, a new type of relationship to the environment (and by extension to an imagined, all-inclusive environment, the universe) developed in a variety of ways. Vitalistic cults gave a ritualized form to human experience when agriculture and cattle-raising came to provide a stable and effective structure for communal survival and expansion. The new vitalistic frame of reference was no longer essentially based on the conflicts between spirits, and in general between warring entities involved in force-against-force situations; it referred to *the cyclic interaction of two universally present modes of operation*—two polarities of a single, all-inclusive "reality" always in motion. This motion, however, was understood to be inherently equilibrated and harmonic; and the purpose of a culture was to establish in a community of human beings a similar type of harmony and balance of power in terms of interpersonal relatedness and fully organized functional coactivity.

This did not mean that all conflicts between spirits, or between the still force-determined, aggressive, and ambitious elements in a community, could be resolved. But vitalistic cults sought to offer means of adjustment in terms of the frame of reference provided by the cyclic and balanced operation of the "One Life" manifesting in the interaction of two great tides of sexual energies.

Biological activity and life's command to "increase and multiply" had been developed in the prehuman, vegetable, and animal phases belonging to the involutionary arc of the great cycle, long before the great reversal of the Noon point. Thus, I refer not to this but to the evolutionary development of homo sapiens and of levels of culture, each of which provides a basic frame of reference for the operations of societies in terms of a fundamental principle of organization.

When the ideal of personhood became incorporated in the vitalistic frame of reference, the concept of autonomous entities responsible for individually definable activities acquired a new meaning. In the new picture, "spirits" were replaced by "individual Souls," and the One Life was replaced by the one and only God who created them. Having become "great religions," the ancient cults were deeply concerned with these Souls which somehow had become attached to human bodies. As a result the human body acquired a fundamental importance. Yet vitalistic cultures gave hardly any value to what happened to *individual* bodies. The biological species mattered, not any one of its specimens. The quality of Life was what counted, not the amount of happiness or degree of well-being of any living organism. The latter always was considered expendable.

B: Transcendental and abstract frames of reference

The vitalistic and the transcendentally religious frame of reference became radically transformed when the concept and the practice of measurement, as well as various analytical processes, were given a place of fundamental importance in culture. Numbers and the simple use of measures in transactions were known long before the classical age of Greece, but a knowledge of the structural meaning of Numbers was considered sacred and reserved to initiate members of "occult Brotherhoods." The men who became known in Greece as Chaldeans were probably not an ethnic group, but members of such Brotherhoods; only at a later time did their name refer to their degenerated followers. Pythagoras probably studied in Chaldean and Egyptian sanctuaries, and there learned most of what he made relatively public in his Krotona school as a knowledge to be imparted only to long-tested applicants who had proven their ability to use the knowledge constructively.

By identifying the successive vocal tones of a magical (i.e. vitalistic) incantation with a series of measurable lengths of vibrating strings, Pythagoras at least appeared to reduce the *tone-quality* of a sound to a *quantitative* value—a number of vibrations per second (the sound's frequency). Numbers, however, did not originally refer only to the counting of "how many" entities or factors were being experienced. Numbers had of themselves a profound meaning as principles of organization; one might say a holistic meaning. The number of factors in a situation, and of phases in a complete process, was in itself significant, irrespective of what the factors or phases were. This meaning could be referred to inherent characteristics of the human mind understood as a universal formative principle; but number deals with the relatedness of everything to everything else. It is implied in the concept of order. The act of measuring constitutes an analytical approach to such a concept. At a vitalistic and holistic level of conceptualization, however, the type of order being studied in analytical processes and in basic measurements is the functional interaction of parts within a whole system.

Numbers originally have a functional character. As they become intellectual entities with which the mind can play, regardless of any experienceable reality in an existential field in which a human person may consistently operate, numbers cease to have meaning in terms of human reality. Yet as products of the rational activity of the human mind, they belong to a new frame of reference which, since the days of ancient Greece, has made "Reason" the supreme principle of organization. The application of this principle to causal sequences of statements or operative processes is "logic." Mathematics and algebra have been developed as special languages to interpret not only experienceable changes but the *logical possibility* of events in situations no human consciousness could possibly experience, even if the human intellect could imagine them.

Logical reasoning and mathematical equations indicate only the *possibility* of such non-experienceable, non-human situations, in terms of the now generally accepted new frame of reference; yet most scientists claim that what is possible is "real." It is real in an abstract sense; but abstraction is confused with universality.

The concept of universality did not belong to the animistic interpretation or even to the early vitalistic levels of human experience, because experience had then a local character. It referred to the responses of an integrated group of human beings to an at least relatively finite field of possible common activity. Travel, commerce, and intertribal marriage extended that field, as did the concept of an area of organized and integrated activity including all human beings and all their possible experiences. Though beyond local situations and experiences, this field came to be understood as a transcendent reality and not merely an abstract possibility.

Greek culture and its diffusion by Alexander's conquests used and glorified Reason as builder of a universally valid frame of reference. But in order to be universally valid it had to transcend the concreteness of experiences conditioned by local features. While the great religious movements of India had given a *divine* character to locality-transcending experiences, the scientific approach of the leaders of Greek culture operated in terms of *abstract* statements. These became rigorously formalized during the European classical age. Abstract formulations in mathematical terms provided not only data of apparently universal validity, but a reliable foundation for the control of material transformations. At first these proved to be extremely valuable in insuring greater comfort and better chances of survival. The ability to *control* became, and today is usually considered, the most glorious characteristic of the human condition. Such an ability nevertheless requires for its operation a definite set of limiting factors. Mankind is now beginning to realize the potential danger of the universal-abstract frame of reference, accepted by an ever-increasing mass of human beings who are unfortunately still dominated by, if not geographically local, at least doctrinally and emotionally divisive religions and cultures. The deepest implications of the worldwide crisis humanity is now facing is that a new frame of reference is needed which can be experienced as a concrete reality. The term *concrete*, however, should be given a broader than physical meaning. The new frame of reference should not only be "planetary" in a geographical sense: it should refer to a being, the Earth-being.

C: The Earth-being as all-inclusive planetary frame of reference

When speaking of the Earth-being I do not mean a globe of dense matter, or a vast organism animated by the life-force, or an immensely powerful and perfect person, or the universal God of the great religions reduced to a terrestrial size. The Earth-being is all these concretely experienceable factors in a total, all-inclusive planetary situation in which the whole of mankind participates. It participates in it, and therefore is able to affect it. The Earth-being is an immense field of activity and consciousness organized at several levels. All human beings operate at some of these levels. The important fact today is that if the meaning and purpose of these operations are understood in relation to the Earth-being as a frame of reference, they may acquire a new quality. Mankind has now to understand what this quality is in a realistic sense, and to accept it consciously, not only as an intellectual or "psychological" interpretation (which may turn out to be an evasion) but as the product of a workable relationship with a concrete Being.

The formulation of what is implied in this understanding nevertheless poses difficult problems. The realization that a workable relationship with the Earth-being can operate at several levels, all of which are "real" yet of limited scope, is an essential factor in the human situation as it has developed during many millenia of history and prehistory. No level of activity can be omitted or bypassed. "Man" as measurer and mathematician has an essential function in the earth-field. He constitutes a level of activity not only in, but of, the Earth-being. How he uses that function and to what purpose are the crucial questions.

The individual and collective interpretation given to personhood in relation to the karma of ancient failures, and the way in which consciousness and human desires approach or respond to the idea of a Supreme Person, are basic issues. The Supreme Person and the avataric beings who are the sources of the various cultures, may

be considered incarnations of an essentially transcendent God external to the universe He created, or
(when the time comes for the potentially transformative
activity) component factors in the evolutionary reality
of the Earth-being. Their Presence in the whole
planetary field is not only an "ideal" interpreted by
various religious systems, but a catalytic (or "in-spirit-
ing") reality—an element necessary to the evolution
of mankind.

This evolution takes place within the all-inclusive
field of the Earth-being's activity and consciousness.
Everything human, as well as sub- and super-human,
should be referred to this planetary field of being. But
this field is not an abstract, mathematically and quanti-
tatively formulatable frame of reference. It is a concrete, multilevel reality to which equally concrete and
multilevel human individuals can totally relate. The
relation is material and molecular, biological in a
functional way, personal in an ecological-cultural
sense, then gradually more and more specialized and
individualized. After a drastic period of reorganization
and transmutation of personal desires, the relation may
take on a super-personal or transpersonal character in
terms of participation in the unified activity and
unanimous consciousness of the planetary Pleroma.
This participation can be, and in time should become
effective in a concrete and realistic sense, if the beingness of the planetary Being is totally accepted as a
"truth" whose self-evidence has become increasingly
objective and unchallengeable. It can be as unchallengeable as a causally linked series of mathematical
propositions, but in terms of another *quality* of conscious response to a situation.

The basic issue is what meaning is given to the word
reality. There is material reality in the explosion produced by the coming together of certain kinds of

molecules. There is biological reality in the nearly uncontrollable mating of a stallion and a mare, or in the
illness resulting from the spilling on one's body of a
test-tube filled with active viruses. There is reality in a
personal initiative which nets social success, fame, or
wealth. But we should not limit reality to this personal,
sociocultural, and financial level of power. Our total
being may be involved in another kind of reality—one
which we not only have to interpret intellectually, but
to which we should respond at a level of beingness
transcending matter, life, culture, personhood, and
even a seemingly incontrovertible feeling-experience
of separate individuality.

If we are fully to understand and attribute "reality"
to such feeling-experience, it has to be given a thoroughly consistent frame of reference. A mathematical
frame of reference may be assumed to be universal
because, being abstract, it is not conditioned by and
attached to any particular experience, but the possibility of any formulation being "universal" in such a
mathematical sense is a highly questionable assumption. This kind of assumption may change. The universality of Euclid's geometry was declared invalid by
non-Euclidean geometry. A pantheistic God could be
considered universal, because He-It would be not only
a creative but also a maintaining factor present in some
incomprehensible manner in every mode of being.
Nevertheless, the belief that a merely human individual
is able *really to experience*, and indeed hold a dialogue
with such a God, implies a situation actually beyond
imagining. It would require the interaction not only of a
human mind but of a whole human field of biological
and sociocultural activity, with a supreme Universal
Being whose beingness extends over billions of light-
years as well as structures the infinitesimal period of
billionths of seconds.

The possibility of such a situation is actually inconceivable, except through the use of symbols (words or
algebraic equations) which can be played with but not
experienced. Yet such situations apparently occur and
produce realistic changes. If they do, can it not be that
they are given a confusing and erroneous interpretation
by the sociocultural mind, and that what is believed to
be "universal," because expressed in abstract and
formalistic terms, is in fact only *planetary*? The God of
the universalistic religions, and the universal "laws"
of mathematically formulated science, may be realities
experienceable at the human stage of culture on this or
any dense planet. They may be "true" in relation to
Man and to the field this Man-stage of the Movement of
Wholeness is able to encompass, and from which it may
extract meaning. The universal constants measured by
modern science may indeed be fully reliable values
"in the neighborhood of" the present level of the human
space of existence which conditions the structures and
boundaries of the human mind. But assuming that they
are universally true may indeed be unjustifiable and a
form of generic pride.

When able to operate at the level of abstractions
opened up through the practice of measurements and
the intellectual correlation of rational thinking, the
human mind can assuredly have remarkable realizations of what it perceives as universal order. The
scientist speaks of "elegant solutions" to mathematical
problems, just as the artist enjoys the "beauty" of
natural or manmade forms, and the moralist is inspired
by the "good" embodied in the fabric of some interpersonal relationships. Greek culture left us the trinity
of the Good, the True, and the Beautiful as a potent
legacy. But each culture has its own definition of these
ideals, even if one may discover beyond the differentiated interpretations and realizations a general

set of "perennial" principles which seem to be valid everywhere and at all times. What is really meant by "everywhere and at all times" are the evolutionary phases of the Movement of Wholeness after the symbolic Noon. These phases refer to the development of personhood and culture, which in turn constitute only a particular level of the total field of activity and consciousness of the Earth-being.

As previously stated, the function humanity has to perform at the level where specifically human situations arise may be significantly interpreted in terms of the neutralization or absorption of the karma of past failures. Such a function, however, has an ambivalent potential; it inevitably includes the possibility of new failures as the result of the "freedom" inherent in human situations. Where and when there is "success," new and more-than-human situations take form as the power of the principle of Unity increases within the field of the Earth-being. Then the development of the planetary Pleroma gradually takes place. This development may become clearer if we use as an intellectual tool the concept of planetary *spheres*—even if today its use is limited to a difference in material conditions.

The planetary spheres

When a geologist speaks of the size or the age of the earth, he has in mind a globe of material substances which he assumes to exist in several continuous states from the surface regions of the biosphere to a central core. This core is geometrically and thus abstractly definable, but whatever reality it possesses does not belong to the field of human experience and human knowledge. The two-dimensional cross-section of the earth-globe depicted in typical earth-science books reveals a circle whose radius is about 6,370 kilometers. The solid surface region—like the shell of an egg—is very thin. Directly or indirectly we know very little of what takes place a few kilometers beneath the soil we walk on.

Below this dense shell of soil and rocky substances a larger region (often called magma) may extend to a depth of some 2,000 kilometers, leading to a core estimated to have a radius of 3,000 kilometers. While the density of the various regions of the globe is apparently known, the determination of the levels of heat and perhaps even pressure to which the materials of the globe are subjected are almost entirely speculative. It has been assumed that the core of the earth-body is made of nickel and iron, but this is very controversial. Actually we have no reliable, direct knowledge of what is at the center of the globe. We have in fact no knowledge of what is at the core of any planet or star. *All human knowledge is surface knowledge*—knowledge referring to changes taking place at the surface of planets and stars. As material inhabitants of the biosphere, human beings are surface beings. Whatever refers to the centrality of being is unknown.

Scientists assume that there is matter at the center of the globe, but they can only speculate on the state of that matter. Yet at the center, there may be "nothing" understandable and still less describable in human terms. A state of perfect equilibrium may be imagined, but beyond what human beings can experience as materiality in terms of the experience of an Earth-being, it may nevertheless be matter. It may be a condition of being in which opposite gravitational pressures neutralize one another—a condition to which Indian seers or metaphysicians may refer when speaking of a *laya* center. It would be easy to think of the core of the earth-globe as the "heart-center" of the planetary Being, but in Kundalini yoga the *chakras* (or energy-centers) are not to be found at the level of materiality of biological processes and organs. These only *reflect* or resonate to corresponding "etheric" whorls of energy. The use of such correspondences, even if intellectually sound, can confuse far more than enlighten.

To speak of the Earth-being as a *living organism* is indeed confusing, because in the total field of experience of such a being, the biosphere—and all that solely refers to "life"—is only one among several levels of activity and consciousness. The biosphere is the place, on both sides of the surface soil of the globe, where the specific features of the biological conditions of existence can develop to their full extent. The lithosphere (rocks and minerals) and the hot magma of the next deeper region of the earth's crust—plus the atmosphere, stratosphere, and ionosphere surrounding the dense and light-obscuring materials of the earth's surface—are all necessary factors in the development of human persons. Personhood adds a new dimension to the field of activity of the Earth-being, but one should not think of the Earth-being either as only a living organism planetary in scope, or only as a person. Whether as an experienceable concrete reality or as an abstract frame of reference for all human situations, the Earth-being encompasses several levels of activity and consciousness.

The first of these is the level of materiality. At that level, the Earth-being is a dense and massive globe made of a multitude of molecules that are complex and integrated factories in which a relatively few atomic elements are continually at work, releasing energy. The next level of being is what is usually meant by "life."

A life-field (biosphere) develops at the surface of the material globe because biological processes apparently require for their optimum actualization the interaction of the *internal* matter of the earth's globe and the many *external* radiations whose frequencies cover a vast spectrum, from ultrasonic radio and heat waves to light, x-rays, and beyond. The boundaries of a field separate that field from its environment, yet they are also the place where inside and outside can meet and interact. Life, as the principle of biological organization using molecular matter as a foundation, is presumably the result of the kind of interactions which have occurred and are still occurring at the surface of the earth-mass.

While this surface region (the biosphere) is an extremely thin layer of activity, its importance in the total constitution of the Earth-being cannot be measured and evaluated in such spatial terms. This importance acquires its essential meaning only when seen in the perspective of the cyclo-circular structure of the Movement of Wholeness, and in terms of the Godhead's purpose for creating a new universe. As already stated, in order to be fully actualized, such a purpose requires the eventual development of human situations allowing the many patterns of ancient karma to become "neutralized," or rather re-absorbed into the rhythms of Wholeness from which a very large number of the components of the humanity of a long-past universe had estranged themselves.

Such a karma-dissolving process cannot be accomplished at the strictly biological level, where instinctual reactions preclude any possibility of freedom of choice. The process requires the operation of the principle of personhood; first within the collective frame of reference of a culture, then in individualized modes of thinking-feeling and behavior. Personhood, however, demands for its concrete actualization a material foundation, as well as the use and at least partial control of biological processes and their derivatives at the level of the collective psychism of a culture. A person unable to resist powerful biological impulses and their translated forms at the sociocultural level (egocentricity, ambition, lust, and greed for material possessions) generates forces and psychic-emotional by-products which fill the realm of the Earth-being to which I have given the name of *psychosphere*. Such a realm may be considered the lower level of the *noosphere*; but the different basic meanings of the two Greek words, *psyche* and *nous* (often believed to be nearly synonymous) should be clearly understood.

Psyche is the human soul operating in the relatively dark regions where predominantly unconscious and compulsive responses are still rooted in biological impulses and organic feelings. In order to deal with the situations produced by these responses, the discursive intellect devises its formalized interpretations through the uncertain chiarascuro of mental processes. *Nous*, on the other hand, is the rational Soul which, for many philosophers and theologians, strictly characterizes the human condition and reveals its divine origin. At the noetic level, human consciousness reaches, or at least should be able to reflect, the archetypal forms previously created by the celestial Hierarchies. *Nous*, when understood in its true nature, is the sphere of principles from which the "higher Self" draws its essential inspiration.

The psychosphere is filled with the often discordant results of the activity of human egos. Interpersonal tensions, conflicts, and frustrations generate a variety of products which accumulate in a repressed, but often still very dynamic, subconscious state in the psychosphere. This level of the Earth-being's existence refers, at least to some extent, to what is popularly understood as the "astral world." It is a "personal" realm in the sense that it is filled with the products of interpersonal relationships. Some of these may be very beautiful, perhaps exalting images of love and happiness; yet they are conditioned by the prototypes, the myths and rituals of the culture. Other contents of the psychosphere are the emotional-mental by-products of culture-shock, collective fears, individual failures of nerve, interpersonal conflicts, tragic disappointments, and biopsychic weariness. An acute feeling of futility may oppress an individual-in-the-making as he or she realizes only too clearly—yet still in a "personal" way not entirely free from egocentric desires and/or expectations—the weakness of his or her position in relation to the masses of so slowly evolving human beings.

The psychosphere acquires a positive character when it opens itself up to the downflow of archetypal images, and the individualized person *accepts* the role of self-dedicated agent for the incorporation of the energies of the noetic realm into a consistent series of artistic, scientific, or sociopolitical achievements. But it should be stressed again that what today is so often meant by creativity is most of the time the result of a yearning for self-expression. In most instances, self-expression follows traditional or recently publicized patterns of organization. The self involved in that activity is usually the ego seeking to achieve sociocultural prestige or to release dammed-up psychic energies. In its most negative and dangerous aspect, the psychosphere is also the field of operation of dark Forces, called *Asuras* by Sri Aurobindo and Mother Mira, "agents of Ahriman" by Rudolph Steiner, and in popular Christianity "devils" or Satanic beings.

Most modern psychologists, eager to operate as psychotherapists and thus as "healers of the soul," find it impossible or unwise to concretize subconscious psychic and noetic processes into post-mortem "astral" entities able to affect (and even to control or totally possess) living human beings, and in some instances a whole crowd of fascinated people. This attitude is consistent as long as the psychologist takes the individual person as a frame of reference for whatever occurs in the inner life and mind of human beings acting within an organized society and its culture. Unfortunately such a systematized approach always tends to over-emphasize the ego level of subjectivity and desires. Similarly, the exclusive concern of physicists with the most easily analyzed and seemingly forever divisible foundation of existence, matter, leads to a kind of reductionism according to which every transformative process taking place in biological organisms and every change in the development of a person has a knowable molecular basis.

If, on the other hand, the Earth-being is assumed to be the most valid and fruitful frame of reference, a much larger picture emerges which allows an all-inclusive interpretation and an effective grasp of the nature and purpose of the situations with which human beings have continually to deal. In terms of such a planetary picture humanity can discover its dharma—its place of destiny. The discoverer is mind. The discovery is the essential *meaning* of whatever is, and of the cyclic process structurally defining the relation of this "is-ness" with all other phases of the Movement of Wholeness.

The full development of personhood does not refer only to the possibility of making at least relatively free and autonomous decisions and eventually to act as an individual who is more or less separate from other individuals as well as from the mass of the people in the environment: it implies the capacity to *extract a meaning* from a series or a group of inner experiences or outer changes.

The concept of meaning may be difficult to define;

but however defined, it deals with the relatedness of any experience within or in terms of a general frame of reference which mind has established. Human evolution can indeed be understood as the progressive development of the human capacity to give meaning to existence, and thus to everything that happens within the field of our planet accessible to human experience. This is the reason for the remarkable ability of human beings to adapt to extremely varied circumstances and living conditions. Such a power of adaptation had to exist as a potential factor in human nature in order for humanity to fulfill its planetary function within the Earth-being. The actualization of that power requires the progressive development of a series of cultures, because each successive culture provides the persons born and educated in it with a specialized capacity to discover and formulate the meaning of its basic experiences. Moreover, within each culture different groups can be educated or inwardly led to give broader-than-average meanings to individual or collective experiences. Any historical event, such as an action starting a world war, can be given meaning according to the psychological state of a particular person or class of persons, to the mass-consciousness and karma of a nation, or to the planetary evolution of mankind.

While humanity's function is to instill the noosphere with the quality of meaning, in the undeveloped state of personhood still conditioned by biological needs and their psychic overtones, many of the meanings extracted from human experiences are drawn toward the psychosphere rather than to the higher regions of the noosphere. The meanings have to be attuned to (or reflect) the realities of the archetypal level if the higher regions of the noosphere are to be developed. A mind that reveals such meanings acts as builder of a foundation for the beyond-the-human level of being which I have called the Pleroma.

In terms of the Earth-being, one can refer to the field of activity of Pleroma beings as the *pneumosphere*. But it may be confusing and unwise to imagine this "sphere" in terms of position and spatial extension. If one does, one might think of the pneumosphere as *the whole orbit* of the earth. This orbit, like those of all the planets, is an ellipse; and an ellipse has two foci. At one of them the sun—the common focus of the orbits of all the planets—is located. The position of the other focus differs in each planetary system. In terms of a geometric kind of symbolism, this second focus may represent the individualizing subjectivity factor in each planetary system; and it should be related in a superphysical manner to the center of the planet's globe. A planet's orbit—its precise shape and position in the series of planets—refers to the function it is fulfilling in the whole solar system (the heliocosm). This solar system represents in symbolic terms the next greater frame of reference for beings whose experience already transcends the planetary and metacultural level.

The Pleroma state to which I am referring operates within the Earth-being; one might speak of it as the "Soul" of the planet. But the word *soul* is quite ambiguous. If one thinks of the Soul as incarnating in a living human organism, the process is involutionary. It refers to the descent of a spiritual entity able to operate in and theoretically to control the biological energies of the body and their psychic derivatives or overtones. As an organization of consciousness and releasable will-power, the Soul is also the result of an evolutionary process, the consummation of personal efforts. Similarly, the activities taking place in the field of operation represented by the archetypal level of the noosphere and the pneumosphere have an involutionary and an evolutionary character. In the first case these activities deal with the impressing and the maintaining of structural patterns of organization (archetypes); in the second case, an evolutionary process is at work through human cultures and individual persons. Its aim is the neutralization of karma and the realization of "meaning." Such an evolution in consciousness is organized in response to the ascendency of the principle of Unity.

When students of quasi-esoteric doctrines speak of the "occult Hierarchy" of the planet, they refer to an involutionary process—the embodiment of the many archetypal aspects of the great Solution envisioned by the Godhead at the symbolic Midnight, and concretized at an "etheric" level in the Supreme Person. The Hierarchy should be thought of as a series of "Offices." Each Office is concerned with a specific kind of structural process through which an archetype is stamped, as it were, upon the development of homo sapiens. A certain type of energy (often called a "Ray") is managed by the beings "performing" functionally in such Offices. In biological terms, the Hierarchy as a whole might be compared to the genetic code directing the activity of molecules within a living cell, or even more to what the biologist Rupert Sheldrake calls a "morphogenetic field." The beings operating in the fulfillment of these hierarchical offices are normally invisible structuring powers, *not* persons; they are "personages" performing an archetypal role in a completely impersonal sense.

In order to perform such roles, these personages should have reached a level of development beyond that of earth-born mankind barely emerging from the biological state of the animal kingdom. Therefore this development had to take place in a pre-terrestrial scheme of evolution—which may mean on another planet or during a cycle antedating that of our present humanity. I tend to believe that at any particular time in a solar system, only one planet provides the conditions necessary for the development of life and later of personhood. The beings who at first perform involutionary archetypal roles as the occult Hierarchy of our present humanity therefore had to be pre-terrestrial beings. A time presumably came, however, when a few individuals who, as products of mankind, had reached on this earth the planetary Pleroma state, were able to perform these archetypal roles or similar functions related to the maintenance and further development of human evolution—and thus to the growth of the Earth-being as a whole.

Reaching the Pleroma state is essentially an evolutionary process. This process takes place over many millennia within a series of cultures; and it involves the succession of many persons, all linked in an increasingly effective degree to a particular "spiritual Quality" which constitutes one of the myriad Letters of the creative Word. It involves going through the difficult and stressful process of reorganization usually called the Path of discipleship, because it implies a two-way process in which the determined conscious aspiration (and imagination) of an individualized person becomes related to the compassionate guidance of a being having already reached the Pleroma state. All Pleroma beings form a partly objective but predominantly subjective "Communion of being," the White Lodge—a Communion in consciousness in which individuality and unanimity are combined.

The White Lodge is not the product of an involutionary process of structured differentiation. Its gradual formation is conditioned by the ascendancy of the principle of Unity. Century after century, culture after culture, human being after human being having successfully undergone the tests of the Path—the rite of passage leading to the Pleroma state—the White Lodge is being "built" (an inadequate term!) as an integrated Company of radiant centers of consciousness and compassionate activity. When considered as the Soul of the Earth-being, the Pleroma may include more than our "human, all too human" minds can comprehend today. As the great cycle of the Movement of Wholeness reaches the symbolic Sunset phase, a new type of situation develops beyond the present state of materiality which generates predominantly subjective experiences transcending what we know today as the condition of planethood.

We can call such a predominantly subjective level of experience "divine"; and we can speak of a state of "starhood" transcending that of planethood. These are speculations and the imagery of minds for which even a planetary frame of reference is too narrow. The basic difference between the type of vision evoked by the all-inclusive Movement of Wholeness and the characteristically religious interpretation of reality is that, in the philosophy of Operative Wholeness, the "divine" state is an integral part of the whole cycle of being, but not an external, utterly transcendent reality. The human state evolves into the divine. The immense multiplicity of human persons becomes increasingly unified. This unification process always has some kind of material basis, but as previously stated, matter is a stabilized form of energy, and energy exists at many levels as do the formative processes of mind.

The human mind interprets the factor of subjectivity as "spirit" in contrast with objectively perceptible "matter." Subjectivity is related to unity (or the experience of oneness), because when the principle of Unity becomes more powerful than that of Multiplicity (after the symbolic Sunset phase when the two principles are of equal strength) the objective world vanishes into predominantly subjective states. To embodied human beings, these states are "spiritual."

In its spiritual state the Earth-being is the planetary Subject. Wherever this subject operates, there is the pneumosphere—the field of Spirit at the level of consciousness of planethood. It is a field of radiant energy beyond the normal capacity of perception of the human senses. Yet one does not have to infer from such a transcendent condition that the Earth-being is a god, or even less, the only God. The subjective factor in the experience of the Earth-being has the potentiality of reaching the divine state as it remains attuned to the momentum of the Movement of Wholeness; but so has the subjective factor in a human being. Of course, a human person operates at a lower level of wholeness than the Earth-being; yet both are "lesser wholes" participating in the field of existence of "greater wholes," and both fulfill a function as participant in the vaster organism. For the human individual this organism is the Earth-being. For the Earth-being it is the solar system or the Milky Way galaxy as an organization of stars.

The factor of size is not what determines the spiritual or divine state. The passage from the condition of individual person to that of Pleroma being does not mean that the person becomes a bigger human being. He or she reaches a state representing a more advanced phase in the cycle of Wholeness—one in which the principle of Unity is more powerful, more able to balance the influence of the principle of Multiplicity. This phase is more responsive to the principle of Unity in the sense that it implies a more profound feeling-realization of relatedness to other beings operating not only at the same level, but at levels below and above personhood. The divine state is not reached as a *separate* individual, even if the traveler on the Path that leads to the Pleroma feels that he or she is tragically alone. The whole Earth-being is involved in his or her success or failure. Yet at the human stage as a subject having gained the power to detach itself from experienced situations, the success or failure is his or her own, because it is related to some ancient individual karma.

This karma had also involved other beings. A mystic may dream of the return of "a one" to "the One"; but this is only the subjective aspect of the process of transcendence. In its full meaning for a human being, transcendence requires that a more inclusive level of being actually be reached—a phase of the Movement of Wholeness in which the principle of Unity is more powerfully at work.

The concept of levels of reality is indeed basic in the whole picture of the cycle I am presenting. Reality is not to be defined only in terms of the factor of subjectivity and the desire for absolute oneness. It is the product of the full triune experience of being, at whatever level an experienceable situation has taken form as one of the many phases of the Movement of Wholeness.

The relation of culture to continent

Every level of activity of the Earth-being is related to every other. The shaping of the materials of the planetary globe at its surface where it reacts to solar and galactic radiations follows rhythms to which present-day geologists cannot give a purposeful evolutionary meaning. Being modern scientists, they build complex and attractive theories, such as the theory of plate tectonics, to explain the formation of present-day continents and their mountains, but they cannot relate the results of the motion of these large masses of matter to the conditions of life which will develop on land or in the ocean—conditions which in turn will make characteristic types of cultures possible. For the geo-scientist, the shapes of the earth's surface— the *geomorphism* of continents and seas—are not related to the development of biology and culture which will occur in the biosphere. There can be no relation because the gradual evolution of matter, life, and culture is not understood as one vast evolutionary process. This process can hardly constitute a consistent and purposeful scheme of development unless it is given meaning in terms of a planetary frame of reference; thus, in relation to an Earth-being in which (or whom) continents, biological species, human cultures and persons participate, each affecting the others to some extent. It is not only that science is concerned with the "how" and not the "why" of existence. The "how" it studies is fragmentary. Only a vision of the wholeness of a whole can reveal the reality of the interactions of its parts by giving them a functional significance.

The biosphere is the first whole to be considered. It includes three main components: the large expanse of water (roughly three-fifths of the earth's surface), the land masses (continents and islands), and the atmosphere surrounded by the stratosphere and still more tenuous layers of substance, reaching to circumplanetary regions filled with electromagnetic particles (ionosphere, etc.). It seems that originally the globe was entirely covered with water, and then gradually masses of molten materials emerged to form what now constitute our continents. When we look at a global map we are used to seeing several distinct continents, as well as names given to several oceans and seas (Atlantic, Pacific, Indian, etc.). Yet in fact there is only one ocean. It is only because we see it from the perspective of the continental regions bordering it that we use different names for this one, single expanse of water.

Land-areas have developed according to the rhythm of multiplicity, but the ocean remains the one basic foundation of terrestrial existence.

In a still more evident manner the earth's atmosphere is one single whole. All living organisms breathe this same air which circulates rapidly around the globe. All human beings are indeed united, in the very depth of their biological nature (in their lungs), by this one atmosphere they have to breathe. We might not wish to have tactual relationships with some human beings of another color, race or class, but we breathe the same air, whether or not we are conscious of or like the fact. Therefore, when a civilization pollutes what it may still call its own atmosphere, it in fact poisons the entire gaseous realm of the biosphere, while the waste-products of European, American, and now Asian factories are filling the one worldwide ocean.

What were once considered several distinct continents may initially have been one single land mass. But traditions and modern theories present several different pictures. The relatively recent theory of plate tectonics has its critics, and the manner in which vast masses of matter have risen from the molten depths of the planet is a controversial issue. Nevertheless it seems evident that continents are drifting and that the geomorphic features of land and sea are very slowly but continuously changing—and some theories give the process of transformation a periodically catastrophic character.*

The idea of drifting continents apparently had been suggested by Francis Bacon and the French naturalist Buffon, but the theory of plate tectonics was developed during this century, at first by a Danish geographer

---

*For a popularized compendium and discussion of the various theories see John White's book *Poleshift* (Doubleday, New York, 1980).

Alfred Wegener. He believed that all present-day continents once formed a huge mass he called Pan-Gaea.
This continental mass then divided into what are now
known as Eurasia, Africa, Antarctica, Australia and the
Americas. Wegener's theory was later reformulated and
two original land masses were postulated instead of
one. The northern continental group centered around
Greenland was called Laurasia, and the southern one
around Antarctica was called Gondwana. As these
two masses moved in opposite directions and (one
might say) attacked each other, heavy geological disturbances occurred such as earthquakes and volcanic
eruptions. Their powerful horizontal embrace gave
rise to vertically surging high mountain ranges. Then
the two masses apparently bounced away from each
other. They remained separated during a long period of
quiescence, and the conflict began again. Several
periods of intense mountain-creating occurred. They
led to the formation of the Laurentian mountains of
Canada about one billion years ago. Another group of
Canadian and Midwestern United States mountains,
now largely flattened, were formed half a billion years
afterward. Then the Appalachian mountains of North
America, and finally (some 150 million years ago) the
Alps, the Himalayas, the Rocky mountains, and the
Andes. This last upheaval occurred during the
Cretaceous Age which theoretically began about 125
million years ago; and it may not yet be ended, as
several mountain peaks (for instance Mount Everest)
are still rising.

The idea of two continental plates moving toward
each other as integral units and colliding rather
spectacularly nevertheless is not universally accepted.
Some geologists believe that what travels from one
region of the globe to another is a number of small
masses breaking off from their region of origin, and

somehow being pulled by and integrating themselves with the much larger land formations. These small wandering masses, imbedded at the margin of continents, are called "terranes." They are identified by geologists because their composition and the fossils they contain do not match those of their geological surroundings. David Howell of the United States Geological Survey believes that the movements of the terranes are "the only process involved at a fundamental level determining the growth and shape of continents." The basic question, however, at least from the point of view I have adopted, is not how the process of formation of our present continents occurred, but the meaning its results have had and are having in terms of the development of the Earth-being *at all levels of existence*—and of course more specifically at the human level. At that level, biology is the foundation of cultures and personhood.

Can we actually relate the shape of continental landmasses and islands to the kind of culture that has developed at their surface? We know how cultures are affected by the climate, the resources of the land and the behavior of all that lives on it, but is there a morphological relationship between, on the one hand, the shape of the land and its location within a continental mass, and on the other hand the type of culture born in that region?

Many years ago, while looking at a map of the world, I was struck suddenly by the fact that what is usually called the European continent, west of the Urals in modern Russia, could be considered a miniature of the much larger Asian continent to which it is attached. I realized that the shape of the land masses at the earth's surface could be related in an archetypal manner to the basic cultures having developed in these geographical areas. I saw Europe protuberating from Asia somewhat as, in a California navel orange, a small replica of the main fruit emerges out of it as a newborn from a maternal womb to which it would remain attached.

The homological relationship becomes obvious when we see that the three basic Asian peninsulas—Indo-China, India and Arabia—are matched in Europe by Greece, Italy, and Spain. Indo-China is prolonged by Sumatra, Java and Bali, somewhat as the Greek peninsula leads to a chain of islands extending as far as Rhodes which could be considered a miniature Australia. On the south of India we find Sri Lanka; on the south of Italy, Sicily. Even the Italian river Po and the plain it crosses can be compared to the Ganges and its region. North of these plains we find in Asia the Himalayas and the Tibetan plateau, and in Europe the Alps and Switzerland. Farther north the plains of Germany match the Gobi and Mongolian deserts. China in the east corresponds to Poland and western Russia, and in the west, Afghanistan and Iran to the *massif central* in France. The shape of Asia Minor reminds us of the rectangular north-south Brittany. The Rhône valley separates the Alps from France's ancient central mountains, as the Khyber Pass separates Tibet from Afghanistan. On the southwestern slopes of the Auvergne mountains an ancient culture many thousands of years ago decorated caves with magical drawings, and southwest of Persia (now Iran), Mesopotamia (now Iraq), Syria, and Palestine were the scene of important historical, cultural, and religious developments. Later on in southwest France a culture, tragically destroyed during the thirteenth century A.D., gave rise to new concepts of interpersonal relationships.

The remarkable fact is that the cultures which developed in the three peninsulas of Asia have characteristics which match those of the corresponding European peninsulas. The central ones, Italy and India, became the sources from which new religious movements flowed in all directions. The Indian emperor Asoka spread Buddhism just as the Roman emperor Constantine spread an institutionalized Christianity. Buddhism took new forms in China, and Christianity became more individualistic in Protestant Germany. The eastern-most peninsula of Asia, Indo-China, was the seat of remarkable artistic developments (such as Angkor Wat) and so was ancient Greece. Java likewise matches Crete in this respect. On the other hand, rugged desert Arabia has been inhabited by a proud race which can be significantly compared to the Spanish people which also conquered large areas of the world in which older cultures were disintegrating. As I wrote nearly forty years ago in *Modern Man's Conflicts*:

> Indo-China with her highly developed art and music, and Java with her rich culture, reminds one forcibly of Greece and the earlier Cretan civilizations. India has been the center of religious doctrines for Asia, just as Italy has been for Europe. The ancient city of Nasik, sacred to Rama, stands (near Bombay) where Rome is in Italy; Benares, where Florence grew. Curiously enough the Arabs settled in Spain (Arabia's structural equivalent in Europe), and both Arabia and Spain are rugged lands, angular shaped, with fanatic, intense, proud populations. As significant are the historical-cultural correspondences between the nations which grew respectively in Persia and in France (Zoroastrian civilization matching the old Celtic culture), in Mongolia and in Germany (military and mystical peoples avid for space-conquest in an organic sense), in China and Russia (lands of the "good earth" and of robust peasantry long controlled by a small aristocracy). (p. 176)

In another sense, of real historical-cultural validity, we might say that Europe is to Asia as the conscious and intellectual part of man's total psyche is to the vast collective unconscious. The conscious is a differentiated organ of the unconscious, in the sense that the brain and the cerebrospinal nervous system constitute differentiated organs of the total human organism. Religion is the progeny of the collective unconscious (Asia); science, that of the rational conscious (Europe).

In such a parallelism differences are as significant as similarities. We spoke of Italy and India, Switzerland and Tibet as occupying similar places in the two geomorphic structures. But we should notice at once the fact that the Alps describe a convex arc of mountains above the Northern Italian plains, while the Himalayas describe a concave arc over the plains of Northern India. If we consider the two mountainous masses of Switzerland and Tibet as the "geo-spiritual" centers of their respective continents, we get the idea of the European center radiating outward, while the Asiatic center is focused inward; and we see how well this describes the difference between the European and Asiatic types of spirituality.

Another way of looking at the Eurasian land-mass is to see it as one shape extending from 10° longitude west (West Ireland) to 170° longitude west (Eastern tip of Siberia). Dividing into two this span of 200 degrees of longitude, we find 90° east as the pivotal meridian; and it passes through Calcutta, Tibet, near Lhasa and near the highest mountain of the globe, just west of the Gobi desert and the Mongolian People's Republic, through a most important part of Siberia (Sibirsk region) and along the great Ienisi river which may become a great trade-route in the future. Around the pivot of this 90° east meridian we might see soon the total population of the Eurasian world almost evenly divided; even now the combined population of India, Persia and the U.S.S.R. balances approximately that of China, Japan, Indo-China and Indonesia. And there is a general similarity of position between the Scandanavian peninsula and Kamchatka, the British Isles and Japan—the correlation between the last two island-groups being particularly significant in terms of world-history and racial background. (pp. 177-178)

It is now usual to speak of seven or eight continents, but I believe this does not provide a sound basis for a geomorphic interpretation of the meaning of land-masses and cultures developing upon them. Asia, Europe and Africa actually constitute one vast, spread-out geomorphic whole I call *Eurasiafrica*. This whole is polarized by the Americas whose overall geometric shape suggests two inverted triangles. The planetary function of these north-and-south triangular masses may be to establish in biospheric and cultural terms a basic dynamic relationship between the north and south poles—the north pole acting as a positive area releasing the global magnetism which may result from the dynamic relationship between the sun and the core of the earth.

The northern span of the two continental masses, Eurasiafrica and the Americas, encircle the Arctic regions, the extensive coast of Canada and Alaska confronting the vast expanse of northern Siberia and Greenland. A chain of undersea mountains in the mid-Atlantic is an eloquent witness to the fact that the two land-masses were once united in one vast continent (perhaps the fabled Atlantis) which, by breaking apart, engendered a basic bi-polarity. The Eurasiafrican Mediterranean sea, on whose shores various cultures grew and the conflict between Islam and Christianity has been and still is staged, polarizes the Gulf of Mexico, which is as filled with islands as the Eastern Mediterranean; and Central America (Mexico included) has been a fertile field for the rise of important cultures and religions. Horizontally elongated Cuba parallels Crete.

Such geomorphic similarities may seem insufficient to establish a causal and teleological link between the recent results of the motion of continental masses and the cultures developing on these areas of the globe. For the same reasons the Medieval doctrine of "Signatures" and the so often mentioned Hermetic principle of Correspondence (as above, so below) cannot be accepted as a reliable basis for data to be used in rigorous scientific thinking. Such non-scientific observations do not tell the nature of forces producing precisely definable results with or against which human beings can work in order to satisfy individual and collective desires for greater comfort, security, and happiness— the implicit purpose of a technology-oriented modern science. They nevertheless pose questions which may sooner or later impel us to adopt a new frame of reference, providing an integrating structure which adds another level of reality to that of the limiting procedures now considered exclusively valid in the acquisition of knowledge.

The basic issue is whether we should attribute "reality" to abstract mathematical relations because they "work" effectively as predicted if applied at the level of the type of matter we can experience. What is implied in their "working"? Atom bombs work; but what value does it have for human beings to know that Einstein's famous equation works if the working destroys the biosphere and the realm of existence at which mankind has a specific function to perform in the Earth-being? Can such a value be significantly called "real"? What is at stake is the *quality* of the type of experiences to which the mathematical frame of reference (as a way of knowledge and a source of activity) gives predictability and effectiveness in terms of material transformations. But *why* does mankind, or a particular society, desire to deal with such situations? It may indeed be that these situations, made possible by the development of the abstract intellect, are desired because another type of situation at a higher, more inclusive level of reality has not been given a correct interpretation. The mathematical frame of reference and its ability to give causal meaning to sequences of events presumably is a valid step in the direction of a superior planetary level of reality. But if its value is glorified above that of all other processes, it may throw out of balance the consciousness and basic desires of a culture. And the results may be tragic. Man may die of "abstractions" in his quest for concepts and formal relations to which modern science attributes a universal character. However, this kind of universality had to be given as a foundation—an ambiguous space-time which, though based on measurement, eludes dimensionality.

Seen from a historical point of view, the restless search of European man for causal "laws" determining the operation and possible use of an energy able to satisfy his always more complex desires, was a revolt against the personalization of the elemental forces experienced as "Nature"—a nature to which, at the time, long journeys were giving an as yet unexperienced, *non-local*, and challenging character.* In fact, the rise of Humanism and the development of an empirical science intent on proving its validity against the authority of a supposedly revealed tradition was not psychologically different from the modern rebellion of teenagers against their church-going but ambitious and profit-greedy parents. The so heavily-praised philosophers of classical Greece were also intellectual rebels against the mythic personification of natural processes in the essentially vitalistic Mysteries which had spread from the East. But transforming the very personal and

---

*The influence of a particular locality during formative years can hardly be exaggerated, insofar as the deep structures of the psyche are concerned.

all-too-human ways of gods into mathematically expressed sequences of events reduced to abstractions
might not be a permanently workable or convincing
solution, however successful the transformation may be
at first in terms of material results.

The frame of reference which I believe may emerge
from the necessity to meet and understand an extremely
dangerous, worldwide situation in which all human
beings are involved includes not only the separately
identifiable levels of matter, life, and personhood; it
refers to their interpenetration in a person-transcend-
ing reality, the Pleroma. When that stage is reached,
the Earth-being may cease to be a globe of dense, light-
obscuring matter needed for the development of
cultures and individual persons; it may glow like a star.
Most people would consider such a possibility as a
science-fiction utopia, not worth thinking seriously
about. Yet what now is indeed a utopia may become
concrete actuality if we deliberately give to its eventual
realization not only our collective thinking and behavior, but also our feeling-responses as individualizing persons aware of the need for a truly new frame
of reference. This new frame of reference may indeed
be the next potentiality which has to be developed
through a slow but consistent evolutionary process.
Do we prefer the mathematical structures that led
Einstein to postulate $E=mc^2$, and the counter-utopia
of nuclear devastation? Before World War II Einstein
had been quoted as saying that he could not conceive
of any practical use for his formula.

It has had a practical use! An uncompromising,
sustained, and transformative belief in the necessity
of postulating an all-inclusive Earth-being as a foundation for the participation and conscious coactivity
of human beings everywhere has also today a practical
use. The crucial issue may be whether this new

frame of reference will have to take the institutionalized form of a more or less rigid "world religion," or if it will embody as much as is today possible of the Pleroma state.

8

*Crises
of
Transition*

Life, culture, and personhood

In order to understand in a constructive manner the general situation which humanity is facing, and to deal effectively and sanely with problems it has been creating, it seems necessary to give an uncommon interpretation to the words *life* and *personhood*, by referring them to definite periods of the great cycle of being. However, what occurs during these periods first has to be clearly understood, and to this end a very brief review of previously outlined processes now will follow.

The reader should look again at the graphic on page 38 which pictures in an abstract manner the essentially circular dynamic structure of the Movement of Wholeness—a basic frame of reference for the interpretation of all humanly definable situations, be they predominantly objective or subjective, material or spiritual. This circular pattern represents the sequence of phases of the cyclic relationship between the principles of Unity and Multiplicity. This cyclic process is symbolically referred to the twenty-four-hour Day period during which the consciousness of a human being normally passes through a relatively complete gamut of experiences in states of wakeful activity in an objective material world, and in sleep—sleep with dreams and beyond dreaming.

Four great moments in the cycle of being are indicated. At the symbolic Midnight the principle of Unity is as powerfully active and the principle of Multiplicity as weak as they ever can be. At Noon the situation is reversed. Moreover Sunrise symbolizes the phase of the cycle when the two principles are of equal strength, but with the trend toward multiplicity and differentiation as a rising, aggressive power. At Sunset the two trends of the Movement of Wholeness are also of equal strength, but the principle of Unity is now the positive, ascending factor in all situations. At Sunrise what we perceive as the material universe is "born." At Sunset it dissolves into conditions of being of a predominantly subjective character.

The half-cycle extending from Midnight to Noon refers to an involutionary process. What was envisioned at Midnight in the Godhead state, as a potentially effective Solution to all the situations left by the failures of the long-ago concluded period of human activity, has to pass from a condition of subjectivity to one of objective and concrete realization duplicating the state of existence in which the failure occurred. The ideal has to become a concrete reality; it has to pass through a process of *involution*.

It does so in several stages: first, within the divine Mind during the period from the symbolic Midnight to Sunrise and in terms mythologized by the actions of Celestial Hierarchies, builders of archetypes; then, after Sunrise, through the differentiation of a tremendous release of potential energy (the Act of Creation) into a variety of explosive whirling motions, stabilized by the still powerful principle of Unity until it eventually becomes the matter which the human senses perceive and whose laws the human intellect discovers in order to satisfy implicit, if not at first explicit, human desires. At last a stage of differentiation is reached when a new level of differentiation and expansion becomes operative, to which the name "life" is given.

The appearance of life on a planet simply means that a further stage of the drive to multiplicity and differentiation has begun. In living cells, molecules multiply and they fulfill numerous specialized tasks. Complexity increases; the potentiality of variations which may lead to eventual failures appears. The processes of life-multiplication, however, reach their maximum of development at the symbolic Noon in the supertropical biosphere of a planet teeming with trillions of biological variations on a relatively few basic archetypal themes. Then, a reversal of the cyclic motion of being occurs. In terms of the cyclic process as a whole, involution ends; evolution begins. The orientation of the Movement of Wholeness now points to the ultimate goal of Oneness. The tide has turned. Life is no longer the dominant factor.

At the spearhead of the forward thrust of the cosmic Movement, a new factor has appeared: *personhood*. The place occupied by life—the end-product of the domination of the drive toward Multiplicity—is now taken by the progressive development of personhood. This development increasingly becomes the most important factor in the half-cycle during which the evolution of composite entities is powered by integrative forces, and a drive toward a simplification of relationships eventually operates. Personhood, however, requires a formative matrix for the unfoldment of its potentialities. A culture provides such a matrix, giving a specific character to the togetherness and the interactions of a more or less large number of specimens of the homo sapiens type. The period of the great cycle between Noon and Sunset refers to the evolution of personhood from a collective stage, still dominated by biological forces, to an individualized state. In that state the personal desires and free will of a "subject" considering itself exterior to the situation it experiences are crucially important factors in the approach to karmic situations, and finally to a process of transmutation of desires and transformation of mind leading to the stage beyond personhood, the Pleroma.

Personhood requires a living organism as a basis for its operations. But this living body in turn needs the activity of material molecules as a foundation for its existence. Both matter and life belong to the involutionary hemicycle of the Movement of Wholeness, while personhood belongs to the evolutionary hemicycle. Personhood therefore develops in a direction opposed to that of life. This development either fulfills the karma-neutralizing function which the Godhead intended, or if negative, deepens the karmic tracks. It may also incite attempts to escape from the path of individual dharma into a subjective dream state, perhaps even leading to a determined and violent regressed state—a state in which the principle of Multiplicity and the energies of life it dominates actively war against the new factor, personhood.

The evolutionary development of personhood would perhaps be, if not impossible, then at least inconsistent and ineffectual, even after the reversal of the cyclic motion at the symbolic Noon, if a mysterious situation did not take place within the Earth-being. This is the concrete presence of the Supreme Person as a radiant embodiment of the Godhead's Midnight vision. The term *embodiment*, however, does not refer to the formation of a body of the dense kind of matter that human senses can perceive. As said before, the Supreme Person's body has substantiality at the highest etheric levels of the physical matter of the earth. But, though this substantial body may not be perceptible except in supernormal instances as human evolution progresses, its presence in the planetary field operates as a powerful catalyst. It is intuitively or psychically experienced by Avatars whose human nature becomes totally pervaded by the power of the Presence, and who henceforth act as channels for its radiance. They themselves become catalysts for the coming together of a few fascinated disciples who in turn father forth a culture.

A culture is a collective way of dealing with matter and life, and of not being overwhelmed by the forces let loose within the planet's biosphere. These forces, however, are active within the biological nature of the members of the culture and they have a tremendous inertia. Even though the direction of the cyclic tide of being has been reversed, the principle of Multiplicity is still the dominant factor in human situations for a long time after the symbolic Noon hour. The set instinctual patterns of the biological level and their psychic overtones—compulsive emotional urges—resist the gradual and effective development of personhood as a means to neutralize the ancient karma. Cultures attempt to limit and focus the power of these biological factors so as to use their energy. A culture may also lead the energy into paths which, denying the natural aim of life-functions, are believed to open the way to a culture-transcending and more-than-human level of experience.

The principle of Multiplicity, though waning, is still extremely powerful until the symbolic mid-Afternoon of the cycle. After the development of human societies begins, it operates mainly in an internalized manner at the new level of the collective psychism which the culture is attempting to build as a strongly integrative force whose purpose is to repolarize the compulsive power of life-instincts. The old biological drives toward differentiation and self-multiplication are given new forms in terms of the development of the ego. While biological instinct is meant to insure survival in optimum conditions of existence in the biosphere, the ego takes form as a composite structure of thinking-feeling and behavior to provide security and the best conditions of existence possible in the family and social environment in which the human being is born and develops as a person.

The newborn and growing child is at first helpless and totally vulnerable in his or her family environment. Gradually, the situations he or she repeatedly has to meet drive him or her as a person-in-the-making to develop a type of mind increasingly able to discover ways of satisfying the desire of a subjective factor which has taken a human character. It has a human character because of the new possibilities inherent in the homo sapiens type of body-operation—particularly the development of a large brain and a sensitive nervous system. Such a type of operation makes possible the detachment of the subjective factor from the experienced situation. This externalized "subject"—I myself, with a particular name—functions as an ego; and the struggle for survival and the will to power that produced the basic law of the biosphere, eat or be eaten, are reformulated at the level of family, society, and culture in egocentric terms. Emotions are aroused and poignant suffering is experienced which is called "personal." These are the results of conflicts between egos, and between an ego and the imperatives that a culture develops and enforces, crudely or subtly, directly (by taboos or a police force) or indirectly (by a sense of guilt and the power of images impressed upon the young child by parents, siblings and teachers). Religious doctrines add their confusion to the situation the child has to face. Their essential aim is to impress upon the child's mind images of a transcendent character—God or gods and the Soul—giving to these integrative patterns the numinous power necessary to insure the stability and unquestionable value of the culture.

These religious images nevertheless appear questionable when a culture begins to disintegrate and the particular aspect of personhood which the culture was meant to develop either has not been fully operative, or has been so perverted (in spite of perhaps spectacular results for a relatively brief period of time) that a new kind of culture becomes imperative. The new culture will be based on a different aspect of the Supreme Person, an aspect which not only will be revealed by a new Avatar and/or a group of avataric personages, but also will be the objective result of social changes caused by the development of new collective powers and new resources.

This evolutionary process leading from culture to culture is not difficult to understand, especially if one accepts the broad picture of the birth and evolution of cultures (or civilizations) outlined after World War I by the English historian Arnold Toynbee. The problem with which one has to deal when speaking of the birth or formation of a culture is to establish the time at which the beginning of the process occurs, and the nature of its preliminary phases. These phases refer to what follows the appearance of an Avatar or avataric group— the mutant seed of a new evolutionary development. The aim of this development is the emergence and eventual stabilization of a basic type of persons, which gives concrete actuality to one of the archetypal aspects of the Supreme Person.

The development of culture and personhood, however, occurs within the biosphere. For a very long time it does not supersede the operation of life-forces. Nevertheless, the essential purpose of the new type of situation should no longer be referred to the trend toward Multiplicity effective before the symbolic Noon. A human being is a person. But when does he or she become a person, and cease to be *only* a living organism? This question is of the greatest importance as soon as one accepts the idea that *being human* does not merely mean being alive, but being a person. To be a person implies being a living organism, but it requires the possibility of operating in situations that are more than biological—*human* situations occurring within the field of activity of a culture.

Plants and animals are living organisms; yet in our present societies and according to the laws of our culture, their livingness is constantly destroyed to satisfy the needs or even the whims of human beings. Whenever such conditions prevail, life *of itself* should not be considered valuable. What is valuable is *human* life; and even the life of some human beings may be judged expendable under specific circumstances. These may refer to a war waged not to preserve the *life* of a people, but their *culture*, their way of life and religious institutions. Recently the issue of preserving "the life" of an unborn being whose parents were members of our human species has acquired a highly emotional intensity; but the problem is inaccurately stated. What is involved is allowing or not allowing the *possibility* of an embryonic life to become a person. After five months of intrauterine development a foetus is certainly alive, but can it be called a person?

People speak glibly of the "right to life"; but what they mean is the right for a person to maintain the operation of the life-function serving as a biological foundation for his or her personhood. There can be no fundamental "right"—that is, the granting of a special status according to the laws of a society and the principles of its culture—to what is *only* alive. Only a person has "rights"; and this person has them because he, she, or (in the case of a collective organization) it is considered a person participating in some manner in the larger system which a culture constitutes.

The issue, however, is so little understood, and what is involved in it is so inaccurately and emotionally stated, that a closer analysis of the factors in the situation seems necessary. An objective approach to the problems it poses should enable us better to realize what concerns the transition between personhood and further evolutionary states open to human beings by virtue of their humanhood.

From foetus to person: birth as initiation into personhood

Being a *living organism* whose specific type of organization and structure belongs to the species Homo sapiens, and being a *person* operating as part of a collective, sociocultural whole are facts that have meaning at two fundamentally different levels. A human being who is not actually able to participate in a society and its culture is not a person. Such a being may be *potentially* a person or *no longer* a person, yet still exist as a naturally or artificially sustained living organism. A human being becomes a person when able to enter into purposeful, sustained, and effective two-way relationships with other human beings within a societal group. Such a relationship implies the capacity to communicate with other members of the group, however primitive the means of communication. Language, not only through words but also in gestures and direct psychic interchange, is the means most specifically used at the level of the human association. Animals—and possibly even cells—undoubtedly have modes of communication through which vital needs and biological impulses are conveyed, but human language has not only a life-maintaining or life-enhancing function; it makes possible the development of freedom of choice between alternatives. These may lead to success or failure; they stimulate or inhibit the conscious and deliberate drive toward a transitional state of being.

A human being can be alive, but still be either not yet or no longer a person. He or she is no longer a person if the capacity to communicate in some conscious manner with other human beings is irremediably lost, as in extreme senility. The mere fact that the heart is beating or that some kind of electrical brain currents are detectable does not make a biological organism a person. In ancient cultures, even the event of physical birth was not considered sufficient to make a person of the biologically operating human child. The child emerged from the *physical* womb of the mother, but until about the age of seven—the "age of responsibility" according to the tradition of the Catholic Church—he or she was not an autonomous and responsible person, able to choose between good and evil. The child's feelings and mental processes were passing through a process of *psychic* gestation within the matrix of the family. In fact, in most societies the definite passage from the familial to the societal level occurred only at puberty. This was because the effective operation of the sexual reproductive function was considered indispensable to the state of personhood— sexual relationship being the foundation upon which characteristically sociocultural relationships could be

built. Sexual relationship led to marriage, and marriage
conditioned, if not determined, the majority of other
purely societal relationships.*

Therefore, the beginning of adolescence was cele-
brated and its crucial meaning dramatically impressed
upon a youth's consciousness. The adolescent boy was
given, or had to discover through challenging experiences, his "spiritual name," in some societies his
totem, and in India his guru. Thereby he became a
person—that is, able to perform a responsible function
in the society and culture which had formed his mind
and ability to act. The adolescent girl also was readied
to fulfill her natural role as wife and mother and as the
binding force within a home and family.

The concept of "human rights" is extremely ambiguous. It is to a large extent the product of the
eighteenth century European mentality and of its extension to the New World. It was an attempt to replace
the religious belief in a God-given individual Soul by
the "self-evident" concrete and objective fact of
existence as a human being produced by two human
parents. But such a fact is given only an abstract meaning if used mainly as the basis for the right to vote or
to be counted as a unit in statistical research. A "human"
right is the right to function as a person within a society
of persons interrelated by a culture, a religion, or a basic
way of life. A man or woman who, unknown to any
other human being, is alone in a vast tropical forest
filled with predators, has no human rights. He or she is

---

*According to the tradition of the Catholic Church, only a sexually
potent human being can be a priest. Celibacy is considered mean-
ingful only if it is the sacrifice (which means also the consecration) of a fundamental power. This consecration is deemed
necessary for the effective transmission of divine energy during
the Mass. Today, however, the principle seems to have been
largely forgotten.

not a person, but only a living organism in an extremely dangerous biological situation. Yet that living organism possesses capacities for adjustment to any biospheric situations which may give him or her the possibility to survive. A seven-month-old foetus that has been prematurely born does not have such a possibility unless it finds itself in an adequate medically supervised environment. A four-month-old foetus out of the mother's womb or of some future artificial matrix has no such potential of independent existence. Yet biological processes have already operated, revealing a potentially human form.

The emotional issue of making abortion illegal on the basis that the foetus is alive, and that the most fundamental human right is the right to life, in most instances is not given a solid and consistent foundation. Several essential questions are not asked: In what kind of human situations can one meaningfully, consistently and practically claim to have a right; and *who* is the holder of the right? How does the idea or feeling of "having a right" arise, and how is it related to a prevailing culture or ideology? Moreover (for the issue has very broad philosophical implications), do we have to infer that whatever is only a potentiality has the right to become actualized?

If one tries to answer the first question, one should first realize that the right to life acquires a crucial importance only where an oppressive social-political system is able, without any restraint, to eliminate persons whose beliefs or actions might cause constant difficulties. The system's right to existence is challenged by the right to life of the person who already exists as a person within the system. In the case of the abortion issue to which the 1973 Supreme Court decision has given a legal and official sanction is the almost unrestrained, egocentric individualism glorified by an increasingly influential host of twentieth-century psychologists and the all-powerful media of a society collectively experiencing the breakdown of its traditional Christian Euro-American values. According to these values, womanhood implied a fundamental subservience to the biological desire of the human race not only to perpetuate itself, but to increase and multiply in spite of the effective power of other life-species (microbes and predators) to thwart such an increase. The human male was meant to fight and overcome the enemies of homo sapiens by physical and intellectual power, while the human female's function was to produce as many human bodies as possible.

This biological situation underlay all types of sociocultural and religious organization until the conquest of the American continent by an eminently aggressive and male-dominated race of human beings. This brutal conquest of enormous land-resources, which the native inhabitants had left nearly untouched, occurred simultaneously with the development of the scientific mentality in Europe, and with the many-pronged attempt to overcome the binding acceptance of the "divine right" of kings and bishops. These events provided the eventual set-up for the uncheckable expansion of the Industrial Revolution. The tremendous growth of industry in turn "dis-biologized" the reality, if not at first the concept and still-official ideal of the family. Women not only had to leave their homes consecrated to the propagation of life, often in order to insure the whole family-livelihood; simultaneously they had to introduce into their natural biological function certain intellect-developing male elements which could only alter their nature radically. Because these elements potentially transcend the biological level, by seeking to achieve absolute sociocultural equality between males and females, the Women's Liberation Movement disbiologized womanhood. It also disbiologized sex; it makes a *personal* issue of the full orgasmic experience of sexual activity.

It had never been such a decisive issue in the traditional Christian European way of life. A "good woman" married a man (most often chosen by the parents for sociocultural and financial reasons) not to enjoy sexual relations with him, and not to "grow" as an individual person outside the experiences which the relationship with the husband and her children brought, but fundamentally in order to fulfill her biological and socio-religious function as sustainer and multiplier of a racial type and of the culture based on that type's biological characteristics. Thus the frequent proscription of marriage outside one's own race and religion or culture.

The abortion issue can be approached objectively and unemotionally only if one sees how it developed out of the human situation outlined above. Another most important factor nevertheless has to be considered: the ability of the recent kind of medical science, based on the male analytical researcher's mentality, radically to alter the average length of the biological existence of a human *body*—a body, not a person. If more bodies are kept alive or made to survive what would have been a disastrous encounter with a predator (now, mainly bacteria and viruses), the strictly biological function of womanhood becomes less crucial. Homo sapiens may increase and multiply without many pregnancies! And because at the same time (an important point!) the socio-financial need for a woman to obtain a job—*as a person and not as a biological organism*—led to the development of the sociocultural and technological mind in persons born female, the disbiologizing and personalizing of sex was to be expected. It has led not only to the crucial attention given to techniques of sexual fulfillment, but to the spread of homo-sexuality.

Sexual fulfillment is a "personal" experience; pregnancy is a biological process. The former inevitably had to be separated from the latter and given the most important role. Sexual permissiveness and the divorcing of sexual results from the biological type of family are direct results of the Industrial and Electronic Revolutions, and of the uncontrolled development and glorification of the scientific mentality. The latter, at the medical level, also made abortion biologically safe and easy, while the egocentric individualism of modern popular psychology and of the Human Potential Movement made it acceptable to at least the surface consciousness of the personal psyche. Today it is said that at least one-fourth of pregnancies in the United States each year (nearly two million) end in abortion. What is more, international organizations for world-population control accept the medical process as a legitimate procedure to achieve an end which has become a crucial human need—the need to stop the uncontrolled proliferation of millions of human bodies kept alive by medical means. These medical procedures *contradict the rule of life in the biosphere*; for in the biosphere, any sudden rise in the number of bodies belonging to a particular species is soon stopped by the increase of predators feeding on or destroying them. Is generalized abortion (and other anti-biological worldwide activities featured by Western civilization as a whole) the predator necessary to reestablish the balance of the biosphere; or is the state of this biosphere to be radically altered and thoroughly "humanized"? Will wilderness everywhere be transformed into gardens to satisfy the socialized and personalized desires of human beings?

The free and generalized practice of abortion may be

called a moral issue, but it is far more than ethical in a cultural-religious sense. It is a planetary issue. The validity of our Western civilization now spreading over the entire globe is an issue affecting the Earth-being as a whole. The devastation of the biosphere (and even of the sublunar regions) by a nuclear war is only one of many possibilities. Overpopulation in its extreme state, expected within the next 100 years, could be (with all its secondary results) just as disastrous. But to speak of it is not considered polite or acceptable to the religious mind, not only at the Fundamentalist or Catholic level of Christianity, but also in India or Islamic countries, because "the will of God" is involved. But this God of theistic religions is the God of Life—who in the Bible is known as the Tetragrammaton, the fourfold IHVH who fashioned the human prototype Adam out of the red clay of the earth-surface. With Abraham he became the god of a special biological line—from seed to seed— and with Moses (or after his partial failure, Moses' successors) the god of a rigid culture and way of life. Even Jesus, who seems to have brought to Western humanity the vision of the "God within"—the God of the free and autonomous individual person—spoke of Him as "my Father." One may assume that the use of the term "Father" was intended only in a symbolic sense; but the mind of the people to whom Christianity spread undoubtedly was operating mainly in terms of biological values, and the Catholic Church could not afford to ignore this fact. It also needed to maintain and increase its power through large families whose members it would physically control from birth.

From the Christian Church's point of view, every human organism has at the center of his or her being— usually symbolized by the heart—a God-created Soul. As a biological organism a man *is* not a Soul: he *has* a Soul. This Soul was believed actually to "incarnate" (i.e. come into "the flesh," *carne*) in the child's body only around age seven, the age of reason and moral responsibility; only then could a child "sin." He or she does not sin *as a body*, but only after becoming a person. Today however, especially in America, children not only develop but are made to develop prematurely under the influence of the cultural environment (above all television) and expectations of the parents who have recently been taught by psychologists that the child must be considered "an individual" at birth and allowed to develop as such. Yet for a long time the potentiality of individualized selfhood can only actualize itself as an ego conditioned by the attempts of the infant's biological organism to adjust to the demands and expectations of its family and social environment. Does the operation of this ego already imply a full state of personhood and legitimate the application of the rights which our culture gives to all persons? Much evidently depends upon how one defines the ego, and whether one identifies this ego with the individual self, considered as the central factor in the state of personhood.

Personhood is an evolving condition of being. It may be an overshadowing potentiality with definable characteristics before it is actualized at the concrete level of everyday existence within a sociocultural setup. And if so, there may be a time when what is still only a potentiality may have to be considered a partially determining factor in the future actuality. It may be that the religious doctrines of the "incarnating" Soul refer to this overshadowing potentiality. In a sense this Soul is the *ideal person*; from a different perspective it is the dharma of the future infant as yet unborn. The overshadowing of the foetus developing in the mother's womb by this ideal form could indeed refer to the phase of the gestation process which is, and especially was, called the moment of "quickening." Today the quickening usually refers to the first feeling a pregnant woman has of movements of the foetus within her womb. However, occult traditions gave a deeper significance to the event: it marked the beginning of a contact between what the future person was meant to achieve and the developing organism within the womb. In the past, this contact was believed to occur when the heart of the foetus began to beat—the heart being considered at least a symbol of centrality of being. Today, however, modern embryologists claim that their instruments can detect halting and imprecise vibrations of the foetal heart-muscles after about one month following impregnation, although a precise, individually sustained heart-beat rhythm is likely to be a different phenomenon. It was said to occur around the midpoint of pregnancy, thus at four-and-one-half months.

If we accept such an interpretation, the midpoint of the gestation period could therefore be the decisive period when abortion would destroy not only the possibility of biological existence as a body, but that of functioning as a person within a human community in terms dictated by a collective culture. A biological organism can be "killed"; personhood may be destroyed. The two processes should be clearly differentiated. Personhood can be destroyed even if the body of the person is kept alive. Today senility means that personhood is no longer operative. If this occurs, the body kept alive no longer has any human "rights" because it is no longer truly "human."

Potentiality and actuality

When considered in the broadest philosophical frame of reference, the problem of human rights thus leads to the question of what meaning one gives to the relation between potentiality and actuality. Does what is only a potentiality of existence have the "right" to conditions making its actualization possible and (what is more important) effective? Can it be treated as if it were an actual and experienceable situation? The impregnation of a human ovum by a sperm undoubtedly produces the potentiality of the birth of a living organism able to become a person and eventually to emerge as an autonomous, self-reliant, and creative individual. But there is no guarantee that this possibility will be actualized. There can be, at best, only a statistical probability. Is such a probability sufficient for a whole community to bestow upon what is only a *future event* the status and "rights" of the state of personhood?

The problem can be illustrated or symbolized by an example from the sociocultural field of music. A composer of serious music is inspired to produce a musical work, either by an internal, psychomental experience or by an external factor—for example, a commission to compose a symphony for a well-known orchestra. The composer's mind is thus "fecundated," and the creative process begins. It may or may not be carried to completion. Preliminary sketches must be written, then an orchestral score. But even the completed score, though paid for, may never be performed.*

Should an unperformed score be considered *music* if no actual sound is heard by an actual public for which it was intended? At what stage of the creative process can the musical work be said actually to exist? Some composers claim to hear the entire music "in their

---

*I personally had such an experience in the 1920s. A work of mine received a substantial prize but was considered "too modern" to be performed. Even recently, similar last-minute decisions by a conductor have occurred due to insufficient rehearsal time, resulting in only a partial performance of one of my works.

head" before even beginning to write the score. Nevertheless, an orchestral score cannot be performed until a copyist extracts parts from it to be read by the instrumentalists of the orchestra. Indeed a number of possible happenings may mar the long process required actually to perform the music in the intended public situation. Thus the musical work can be evaluated only when it is related to a sociocultural group of people. It is only within such a group that a composer could possibly claim the right to hear the actualized sounds to which he or she had only given the potentiality of existence.

Moreover, what is potential may not be worth actualizing, at least from the point of view of the directors and the expectable conductor of the orchestra to which the potential music (the orchestral score) has been sent. If the orchestra had an infinite amount of time and resources, all potential symphonies could be actualized (i.e. performed). But in a finite musical season—and at a cosmic level, in a finite universe—*all* possibilities cannot be actualized. Someone, or some factor, has to choose.

According to the picture of the cycle of Wholeness I have presented, the choice is being made by the karma of the past. The ancient failures condition a dharma having the power to neutralize or balance the karma they engendered. The supreme Compassion of the Godhead at the symbolic Midnight of the cycle takes the form which, through a new set of human situations, will give the best chance of readjustment to reawakened subjective centers that once had been thrown out of the rhythm of the Movement of Wholeness by the pull of disharmonic desires and the destructive use of power.

If, however, we return to the problem of the termination of pregnancy, what is involved is certainly *not* the actualization of a potentiality of personhood inherent in millions of similar *biological* occurrences, but the relation of this situation and its equally potential results to a much more inclusive *interpersonal and sociocultural* situation. To say that a woman has the right to dispose of what happens to her body is quite beside the point. Does not our society interfere with a person's desire to commit suicide? Does it provide the sufficient amount of biologically wholesome food to children of all families if the parents are jobless? At the biological level, the human species is far more important than any one of its members, and the character and quality of the cultural-interpersonal organization of a society is more crucial in the spread of abortion methods than the individual reaction, dismay, or fear of an unwillingly and unexpectedly pregnant woman.

Sexual permissiveness is the symptom of a collective situation in which a culture has lost its capacity to make evident the need for the controls it previously imposed upon the unhindered play of biological impulses. As the rhythmic power of the cultural processes of human evolution fades out, as the options for superficially self-determined patterns of change multiply and none seems sufficiently compelling to produce an enduring commitment, the impulsion to depend again upon pre-cultural biological stimulation inevitably spreads. The often empty or tragic results of this adolescent protest, given psychological legitimacy as a personal attitude in terms of supposedly mature relationships, may lead to a panicky return to old, seemingly stable and secure traditions in the name of morality and monogamous commitment. But remember the often quoted words of the first person to reach the summit of Mount Everest, when asked why he had done it: "Because it was there"—in other words, because he felt that what was only potential had to be actualized.

The human situation is undoubtedly characterized by the drive to actualize what is only potential. This is human greatness but also the source of human tragedies and failures. The development of the human person, and collectively of a human culture, may reveal paths open in many directions. But during the long ages which see the rise of more and more complex cultures and personalities, the most significant and valuable thrust of the Movement of Wholeness is the drive toward greater inclusiveness and concentration. It should be in actual practice a drive away from the multiplicity of surface-experiences and eventually to the attainment of a state of centrality in which all circumferential possibilities are unified in equilibrium and peace, in simplicity and harmony.

The road to that all-inclusive peace of center requires the control of many options, the refusal of many possibilities. Thus culture sets limits to biology. Personhood rises out of life, but is born of sacrifice—in the sense that it can give a "sacred" meaning to life-impulses by making them symbols of a superpersonal, planetary, cosmic, or divine reality revealing their essential function in the cyclic process of Wholeness. It can also, alas, give an anti-sacred character to these biopsychic urges by enslaving them to an imagination always eager to discover new possibilities and to make them actualities out of tune with the tide of cyclic being.

The process of individualization

What emerges from a material womb is a biological organism of the homo sapiens variety, requiring for its survival to be fed and cared for. Even though it differs in outer features, biological temperament, and molecular chemistry from other newborns having a similar genetic ancestry, it cannot be called "an individual" in the common sense of the term. Nevertheless it has the potentiality to develop individuality within the psychic matrix of family environment and culture. From the point of view already established in this book, this "individuality" is the type of personhood which has the inherent possibility of successfully meeting and neutralizing the karma (or unconscious memory) of past failures. It is the dharma for the fulfillment of which the newborn human organism was formed and is now growing in a particular milieu. This milieu is basically the very kind of environment which will make the dharma fulfillment possible. Such a possibility, however, may entail many difficulties and much suffering, through which the karma will take concrete experiential forms. As the person is born who sooner or later will have to meet and interact with the karmic residua of the past, the birth-situation brings together three basic factors:

1. A family environment and its culture, way of life, and religious beliefs focused by the character of mother, father, and other participants, animate or inanimate. This environment is structured by the collective values of the culture and the social class and wealth of the parents, but it is also affected by their biological temperament and personal character. This family environment imposes upon the growing infant's organism numerous constraints considered essential to a successful process of growth.

2. The infant organism nevertheless operates instinctively according to the biological rhythms of its functions. These rhythms in many ways conflict with the patterns which the culture and the family-group believe to be correct procedures in the baby's upbringing. "Something" in the baby develops as the result of such a conflict. This something, the ego, is formed as a means to adjust as effectively as possible the biological impulses of the infant to the demands of the family

environment and the culture prevailing at the time and in the circumstances of the birth.

3. This process of ego-formation is possible and takes on a special consciousness-engendering character in a human baby because it is a member of homo sapiens. Such a life-species could appear in the biosphere because the symbolic Noon phase of the great cycle of being had been transcended, and the influence of the principle of Unity was slowly ascending. It was made possible by the concrete Presence of the Supreme Person as a new factor within the Earth-being. Dimly as it is felt in the depth of human beings, this Presence catalyzes an unconscious urge to rise from the biological level to that of the Pleroma, *through* the trials and difficulties of the individual level of the state of personhood. Only in this state can the neutralization of past failure through the exercise of "free will" be performed.

In primitive biologically-determined animal groupings and societies, the adaptation of a living organism to the conditions prevailing in its birth-locality is apparently compulsive and unconscious; instincts rule, unchallenged. In a human being, however, the development of conscious and deliberate patterns of adjustment to family and sociocultural constraints is not only possible, but almost always occurs when a particular level of the evolution of culture is reached. Instinctual adaptation to the dictates of a tribal system based almost exclusively at first on survival and self-reproduction is replaced by conscious ego-determined behavior.

At the ego level, biological temperament becomes personal character. This character is a compromise between biology and culture. It defines a particular way of being a person in a sociocultural environment. What was at first a mostly *collective* type of personhood, subservient to the taboos and way of thinking-feeling and behaving of the culture, becomes an *individualized* type of personhood through the operation of an ego.

The formation and activity of an ego is inevitable. But the ego-forming process may be overpowered by the principles of organization, customs, and laws of the society, and by the development of a binding power, the collective psychism of the tribe. It may be overpowered by dominant and possessive parents or associates. On the other hand, the ego may develop in an atmosphere of conflict and violence when it strenuously resists the pressure of family, religion, and culture. Then, refusing to adapt and compromise, it finds specific ways of proving itself different and unique. A person controlled by a strong ego acts, thinks, and feels as an "in-dividual" because this ego is able to mobilize and control the psychic and even biological energies of human nature in an "un-divided" manner. The individualized ego-controlled person in most instances still operates within his or her native culture, but has emerged from the psychic matrix of family and culture as a relatively independent "individual self."

The basic issue, however, is the conscious purpose and the quality of this emergence. What gave it the character it has taken? How will the by-products of the separation from the family and cultural matrix, and perhaps the embittered or lonely isolation from the natural and natal environment, be handled? Where will this new feeling-realization of being radically different from the more or less rigidly organized masses lead? During a period of cultural disintegration, what will result from the alienation of the person eager for spiritual transformation from the free-for-all struggles of egos seemingly eager to destroy any natural patterns of order and relatedness so as to prove their freedom and power? Is this feeling of "being different" to be considered the means to demonstrate the superiority of a free and perhaps creative individual—the man of power, the woman star, idol of the masses, the revered genius or inventor, and in general whoever demonstrates the triumph of the human will over nature—or is this process of individualization and overcoming of bondage to both biological compulsion and sociocultural imperatives only a transitory phase in human evolution whose aim is to produce the conditions necessary for the neutralization of karma and to lead to a still more basic kind of emergence? And, if the latter, what kind of emergence? It should be that of a karma-free being—one among thousands of other components, ready to participate in the activity and consciousness of a super-individual and super-physical whole, the Pleroma, the Soul of the Earth-being.

The process of individualization begins in the formation of the ego, but the patterns of the ego (its *modus operandi*) are still basically conditioned by the demands and constraints of the culture. These, however, establish a frame of reference—and symbolically speaking, a psychic womb—necessary to define the potential structure of the individual-in-the-making. A mason builds a physical structure, as it were, against gravity; individuality takes the form it needs to take against the pressure of the collectivity, because the particular collective culture in which the human being is born provides optimum conditions for the reawakening of the memories of past failures through sociocultural situations making possible the solution of the karmic problem. Personhood, I repeat, is the overall Solution envisioned by the Godhead in the Midnight phase of the cycle; but this Solution has an immense number of aspects because the components of a person's humanity had failed in an equally immense variety of ways. The family environment and the culture in which a person is born represent the person's ancient past in its essential or symbolic form insofar as this past included karma-engendering sins of omission or commission. Individuality takes form against this karmic pressure. If the mind of the individual-in-the-making can understand and accept the situation, and if his or her desires (the subjective factor in the experiences being evoked by the life-situation) do not cling to old biological patterns, the karmic darkness can be transformed into light—the light of accepted meaning.

When the purpose of passing through the state of personhood is revealed and assimilated, a further period of the evolutionary process opens up. The principle of Unity has become more powerful, nearly equalling in intensity the principle of Multiplicity. The latter has been retreating inward, but its inertial strength is sufficient to affect weak or desperate persons. The conscious and deliberate movement toward the radiant Pleroma state may find its shadow counterpart in several ways: in an utterly weary falling by the wayside, in an escape into a subjective dream state, or in the noxious disintegration either of persons who would not dare to be individuals, or of individuals whose desires and minds could not meet crucial situations except in terms of personal fulfillment in a culture or of individual separateness.

The process of individualization is an emergence out of the state of unquestioned subservience to the paradigms and religious beliefs of the society in which one is born and where personhood has developed. While the first stage of the process is the formation of an ego, a further step leads to a contact with the dharma that defines the purpose of the birth. I have spoken so far of this dharma mostly as the means to neutralize the karma of the past. But beyond this process of neutralization, the consciousness of the individual struggling through the process of liberation may already have an intuitive sense of the place and function he or she will fulfill in the next transcendent and planetary state of the Pleroma—provided that the "spiritual Quality"* vibrating at the innermost core of his or her personhood succeeds in drawing and attaching to itself the so often vacillating desire and will of the individual on "the Path." As this occurs, the individual is not lost but operates within a new frame of reference which includes the whole of humanity and the Earth-being of which it is a part. Personhood—in the strict sense of the term—vanishes, having served its purpose as a means to solve the karmic problem. Then at "the end of time" the prototype of personhood, the Supreme Person, is released—or perhaps it is absorbed into the many individuals who have successfully passed through the often tragic rite of passage beyond personhood. The theosophical tradition speaks of that end of time as "the Great Day Be With Us." On that Day, unanimity and individuality interpenetrate and combine into the Pleroma state of being. Unity and Multiplicity are balanced, and a new level of beingness begins at which the subjectivity factor increasingly dominates the experiences which metacosmic situations now provide.

The path of discipleship

In the process of individualization, there is an emphasis on whatever makes the would-be individual different from his or her family or peer-group, and especially from the masses that unquestioningly follow the patterns of their culture. The result is a state of at least relative isolation. Discipleship, in the broadest sense of

---

*See *Rhythm of Wholeness*, chapter Five, page 97, for a definition of spiritual Quality.

the word, implies on the contrary a new state of relatedness. The disciple is related to his or her master or
teacher, and in many if not most cases, to other disciples. Discipleship is a shared relationship; and this
relationship may be to a common ideal or set of beliefs
as much as to a superior personage, whose superiority
may be one of physical or mental skill, or of state of
being and consciousness.

Discipleship implies not only relationship to a
superior being who has accepted the relationship; it
requires that the disciple either ceases to be busy
stressing his "difference" as an individual while learn-
ing to respond to the vibrations of a higher state of
being, or is able (and perhaps inwardly directed) to
use that difference, as well as he or she can, in terms of
the type of purpose characterizing this higher state. At
the level of social, artistic or business productivity, this
second alternative would result in team work consciously pursued in terms of a clearly understandable
material purpose. But, at least during the earlier stages
of the spiritual Path of discipleship, the basic concern
is not what the group of disciples may be able to produce objectively, but rather the use of the tensions
inherent in the interpersonal relations between the
disciples, in order to intensify the process of transmutation of desires and the transformation of the mind.
Not only the desire for personal achievement, fame, or
wealth—and perhaps for special favors from the master
—but even for a strictly individual existence, has to be
transcended. It should be replaced by faith and a deep
sense of potential, even if not yet actual participation
in a planetary Communion of beings. The mind has to
open itself to concepts and quasi-visual experiences
which inevitably seem paradoxical and non-rational to
the culture-built intellect of the disciple.

At the level of the traditional guru-chela relationship

in Asian and Near Eastern regions, the chela was expected not only unquestioningly to obey the guru in terms of behavior, but to condense and unify all the currents of his or her psychic energy (thus his or her entire emotional life) into a single stream of devotion (*bhakti*) to the guru. This unifying process can be related to what is expected in the practice of Kundalini Yoga, that is, the drawing of the life-energy away from the cells of the entire body, then the condensation and the rise of that energy along the central channel of the spinal column until it reaches the Ajna chakra behind the forehead. There the energy is said to unite with a descending current of transhuman power. The power of the Pleroma "descends" *through* the guru to transfigure the chela whose whole being has become an integrated musical instrument able to resonate to the super-cultural planetary rhythm of the Soul of the Earth-being.

When, during the sixth century B.C., the consciousness of the vanguard of mankind became ready for the development of a new level of mental activity, Gautama the Buddha, Pythagoras, and other great personages attempted to give a public formulation to the new mind. As a result, it became possible for the process of transition from the cultural and individual state to the Pleroma condition of being to take a new form. Some early theosophists spoke of a "reorganization of the White Lodge" at the time of Gautama; and according to the German philosopher-occultist Rudolf Steiner, the impregnation of the matter of the earth by the blood of Jesus at the crucifixion made possible a basic change in the process of Initiation.

Such statements may best be interpreted, I believe, as more or less symbolical indications that some twenty or twenty-five centuries ago a new level of operation of the human mind and of the psychism a culture

generates was reached *as a worldwide public possibility.*
A possibility only. The archetype of a new rite of passage having been released, a new elite of mentally
mature human beings, ready to experience the transition between personhood and the Pleroma, could do so
in terms of an individualized, mentally formed consciousness, rather than solely at the level of the control
of biopsychic energies. As a result, karma can now be
understood as a significant and symmetrical cyclic
process instead of as the operation of a blind and meaningless force of Nature. Only a fully developed individual self is able to give a series of karmic developments the meaning of tests of liberation revealing the
Compassion of the Godhead. This self alone may
intuitively feel the great rhythm of the Movement of
Wholeness, even through apparently disruptive and
challenging events experienced along the Path. It has
to be a self fully accepting the responsibility of the
state of individuality and of the freedom it entails,
rather than making a mysterious, essentially transcendent, and incomprehensible God the cause of
suffering and tragedy.

A successful transition to a state of being beyond the
merely human requires more than a new type of mental
process. What is needed is a repolarization of the experiencing subjective self. There must be a shift from
an isolated and strictly individualistic state dominated
by the principle of Multiplicity to the field of attraction
of the principle of Unity. And this implies the transmutation of the person's basic desires. These changes are
possible because new situations and new relationships
arise, releasing an at least partially supernatural surge
of potency. The whole being of the traveler on the Path
is gradually (and alas often very painfully) experiencing
a process of deconditioning, then reorganization. Because the principle of Multiplicity is still very powerful

even in predominantly subjective states of being, each person who reaches the level of mentally aware and intuitive individual selfhood is confronted with the way best fitting his or her "difference." Yet the process has an invariant foundation which has to be accepted in every case. No basic step can be missed, for its avoidance would leave a karmic shadow that might later lead to a more crucial failure.

To the religious spirit this means that God's Will must be accepted unconditionally; but on the Path of transformation, more than a passive acceptance is demanded of the individual traveler. As it has often been stated in inspirational semi-esoteric writing, he who ever treads on the Path eventually has to become the Path itself. There is no escape *from* what one is as an individual; only a victorious passage *through*. The defeat of a resurgent army of ghosts, vividly remembered as reawakened images of what one had been can alone lead to the Pleroma state; and the elation of success must always be tempered by the humility born of the realization that victory could always have been more complete.

It is futile to reduce the Pleroma state of being and its combination of unanimity and individuality to patterns operative in our sociocultural, political, and business world. It is also futile to personify seemingly individual sources of radiant power and Compassion that ignore our commonplace sentimentality. Nevertheless, even a tentative knowledge of the nature of a basic process of metamorphosis may be valuable, because the quality of livingness of human persons attempting to tune up to the oneward Movement of Wholeness often depends on the conscious understanding of what is at stake. As individualized human persons we have a right to understand—a right to meaning. This indeed is the basic human right, rather than an ambiguous right to life, happiness, and other bland achievements. The spiritual life is a series of victories; the reward is always a more inclusive understanding of what one is meant to be—a deeper, fuller, richer experience of Wholeness.

How to deal with changes of level

The first change occurs when the newborn organism begins to participate, unconsciously though it may be, in a system of communications primarily aiming at biological survival, yet controlled by the specific behavior patterns of a culture and a particular family situation. Cries, gestures, and changes of facial expression are the original means of communication available to the baby reacting to ever-changing internal and external situations. As it is being trained as a biological organism within a somewhat rigid cultural system, the infant has to develop an ego in order to make the most of a confusing, yet (it soon realizes) repetitive series of situations to which he or she has to conform.

What begins at birth acquires an increasing complexity as the years pass. The child is being "encultured." The process is called education, yet it actually refers to a series of instructions. A set of expected correct reactions and a vast number of memorized data are "built in" (*in-struc*), producing an increasingly complex network of cellular interactions in the child's brain and nervous system. These interactions define the ego, the first manifestation of personhood. The function of the ego is to make the demands of the family and school environment as comfortable as possible to the biological organism. Furthermore it is to use the expectable reactions of family members, teachers, and playmates in a way which enhances the power and increases the possessions of a psychic entity asserting itself as "I," Peter or Jane. The ability to imitate patterns of behavior is the first requirement during this process of enculturation and ego-development. Imitation (or mimesis) results in organismic pleasure and in an increased acceptance by surrounding people. Memory and discrimination are needed effectively to deal with the situations being met. Important also is the ability to sense, feel, or intuitively realize what adults and even siblings and playmates will appreciate or resent. These qualities (memory, discrimination, and empathy or intuition) are not only needed in childhood; the process of instruction extends, or at least can extend, to the entire life-span. However, the process of individualization takes on a new quality whenever a factor introduced in the relation between the growing person and his or her family and culture is given a determining influence. This factor is the transformation of mimesis into revolt *as a way of growth.*

At the level of depth-feeling reactions, the breakdown of a quasi-instinctual devotion to parents, and of an unquestioning acceptance of the validity of assumptions and practices embodied in the family religion, inevitably produces a crisis. It is a crisis of identification rather than identity. While it has its roots in the series of reactions which resulted in the formation of the ego, what is at stake in such a crisis is not merely the convenient adjustment to a set of situations, but rather the forceful assertion of an individual identity, I myself, and all this possesses to substantiate this "me." And of such possessions none may seem as essential (at least to Descartes!) as what is now definitely considered to be "my" mind.

At first, however, the deep sense of identity operates almost exclusively as a "gut-feeling," rooted in the wholeness of the body and the organizational power of "life" keeping all its cells integrated. This feeling

establishes the way the I, as a person, manages to keep
alive and relatively happy in the sociocultural environment in which it has to function. But behind the obvious
ego-feeling, a still deeper yet much less focused awareness of a "purpose" for being-I may occasionally
surface. Mind often integrates and formalizes this
awareness in answer to a usually imprecise, yet perhaps
haunting desire to discover the meaning of sufferings
and deprivations, and perhaps a still more basic meaning to human existence in general. As this occurs, the
concept of dharma may arise (however formulated) in
the consciousness. The question is then not only "Why
does this happen to me?" but "Is there behind and in
'me' a power able to act in trying circumstances so that
a new level of consciousness and activity may be
reached?" It could be a higher, wiser level of personhood. It could also be a level of being whose roots and
source of potency are *beyond* personhood, even though
it may still operate *through* personhood—thus "*trans-
personally.*"

At this point what is called "the will" should be dealt
with—a factor characteristically almost ignored in
twentieth-century depth-psychology until Dr. Robert
Assagioli devoted a whole book to the subject, *The Act
of Will.* The will, however, can be given an exalted
spiritual meaning it does not have of itself. It operates
at several levels, just as the feeling of being-I and the
desires it engenders do. I have defined the will as the
mobilization of the energy factor in the satisfaction of
a desire aroused by a particular situation. Desire itself,
as noted earlier, is the expression of the subjective
factor in all experiences. Any experience implies a
conscious or unconscious desire for or against some
expectable event, or else a condition of indifference.
The more intense the desire, the more potent the
mobilization of the energy it releases, provided that the

mind—whether in its cultural-collective or its personal-individual aspect—either provides an effective channel for the power, or at least offers no insurmountable obstacles.

The character or quality of the will depends primarily on the level at which the desire calling for the mobilization—and therefore the subjective source of the desire—operates. The subject may have a generic and biological character—such as a whole species manifesting its desire for food and copulation in and through any one of its particular specimens. It may be a collective factor—a nation seeking territorial conquest in and through a military leader, emotionally and mentally controlled by the vision of power his environment had indelibly stamped upon his personhood since infancy. The subjective source of the desire may be an ego fighting for self-assertion at home or for a superior position in business; and in that case an ego-will is at work. This last alternative is the most frequent in our individualistic society—a society of egos, by egos and for the greater good of egos!

Ego-will may use many methods of operation in order to achieve its basic but multifarious aim: the control of natural forces for the satisfaction of human desires. Natural forces may be implicit in biological functions (as for instance the sudden tension of muscles) or they may result from alterations in the relation between external substances or beings. An instinctual arousal of such forces is transformed into ego-will when it is made to occur deliberately and according to a set series of operations (a technique) consciously worked out by the mind. The human mind is therefore a most important factor in the effective activity of the ego-will. This mind takes on an increasingly human character when the subjective factor (I, Peter or Jane) considers itself separate from the situation it experiences. But if this ego-I is external to the situation, so is its desire for making the situation develop in a particular manner.

The desire for making a situation change into another expected to bring comfort, happiness, wealth, professional prestige, or political power is a dominant factor in the process of individualization. At the *collective* stage of the development of personhood a human being acts much like a cell in a biological organism, fulfilling the function that he or she was born for—a function determined by the conditions of birth as a human body. The *individual* stage of personhood develops when the character, the unusual capacities and/or performances of a person, singles out and brings him or her to a position of eminence.

The less dependent upon strictly biological patterns of relationship and the more individualistic the society, the greater the possibility for a participant in the societal process to reach a position of dominant power. The mobilization of the person's energy, according to methods devised by the mind, assumes the character of ambition. What, in a normal happy childhood, had been the devotional will to please the parents, born of the desire to love and be loved, becomes the ambition to gain an individual position of power at one level or another of the society. It is still the same will, the same ability (or inability) to mobilize internal energy, or to control external forces and the situations they produce; but the level of operation and the quality of the subjective factor have to change if collective personhood is to evolve into individual personhood. The change, however, may be a smooth and easy process, or it may require a sharp and painful crisis of revolt and severance in order to pass from one level to another.*

---

*The section of the booklet *Beyond Personhood* entitled "Three Lines of Development of the Ego" discusses various possibilities of development of the feeling of being a "special" person within a sociocultural environment.

The relinquishment of the ambition motive usually results from experiences which reveal the inefficacy or illusive nature of situations which a special condition of birth and education, or a tense ego-will able to control sociocultural and interpersonal processes, had produced. A buddha is shocked by the revelation of human situations he had never been allowed to know; an ardent and relatively successful leader of a political revolution is made to face the utterly disappointing results of changes his will had made possible; a man whose desires drove him to constantly repeated and ever cruder or more refined sexual experiences sees his life and the culture that spurred him on as totally empty. Faced by such a situation, a person may collapse into a state of indifference in which the exhaustion of his desires engenders a revulsion against all that mind has devised as a servant of desire and inventor of ever new procedures for the realization of ambition or more intense pleasure. The revolutionary may fall back with a more or less hidden sense of defeat to the anonymity of social and personal normality—perhaps only a temporary step to regather a new sense of potency mobilizable when a new cycle of change begins, if it ever does. But something else of a positive nature may occur. An as yet unknown or long ago dismissed type of realization may make an unexpectedly strong impact upon the consciousness of the weary person ready to disavow his or her unique individuality; and a process of reorientation and repolarization of the subjective factor may begin, which should lead to a transmutation of desire and eventually to a new will.

As a third factor inherent in experience, mind deals with procedures. It seeks to ascertain how the basic desires of a whole collectivity of people or an individual person can be satisfied. The procedures being sought evidently are based on the interpretation which the mind factor gives to the situation; but this interpretation assumes the validity of a subjective state of being. Consciousness, on the other hand, refers to the direct "prehension" (rather than comprehension) of the wholeness of the situation being faced. As I stated at the beginning of chapter four ("The Human Situation"), consciousness is an aspect of Wholeness or Beness. It operates at several levels as the emanation of the then-prevailing particular state of relatedness of the principles of Unity and Multiplicity. Thus one should not speak of the consciousness *of* a human person (or a plant), but rather of consciousness *taking form within* that person (and plant) as each meets at its own level a particular type of situation. Every situation in the vast cycle of the Movement of Wholeness implies the potentiality of a particular mode of consciousness. This type of consciousness is inherent in the subjective factor operating in the experience the situation makes possible.

Consciousness, operating directly within (or, in a sense, as) the subjective factor in a human experience, is what should be meant by the much abused and misused word *intuition*. Intuition is a subjective awareness of the wholeness of a situation "seen" as a concrete manifestation of the possibilities inherent in a particular relationship between the principles of Unity and Multiplicity. Intuition opens the door, as it were, to the realm of Wholeness—to the essential reality and meaning of what is, was, or will be. At the level of human situations, intuition is diffuse and imprecise revelation of the dharma of the person in whose consciousness it takes form. It reveals not only what a perhaps imminent situation may be, but also the meaning of this situation in terms of the basic evolutionary purpose of the state of personhood. Intuition suggests to the individual, perhaps vividly, the degree of acceptance or avoidance of a situation which best fits the purpose of his or her being a person; thus what the value of the desire related to it essentially is. Intuition may reveal the possible conscious use of the situation in the process of neutralization of past failures. It may also operate when the decision has to be made whether to carry further or delay awhile a series of successful moves along the Path of transformation.

Intuition is therefore a faculty particularly needed when the process of individualization leads to the possibility of making crucial choices which might increase the feeling of separateness and pride. It enables the individual whose over-defined subjectivity is functioning, as it were, outside the tide of Wholeness, to respond to the oneward thrust gaining strength as human evolution proceeds in the direction of the symbolic Sunset phase of the great cycle. Intuition, however, needs the support of two other essential factors during crises of transition: imagination and faith.

In the precise sense of the word, imagination is the faculty mind possesses in varying degrees to produce images evoking the possibilities of relations and experiences which, under the pressure of circumstances or internal factors, may be desired, but are not actualized in the present situation. These factors may have been actualized in the past and the person may desire their revivification; they may be a play of the mind seeking to help the subject escape from inner emptiness and estrangement from the state of evolution and the level of thinking-feeling his or her environment features at the time. These images may also be evoked by an imprecise and confusing feeling-awareness (or intuition) of what might have been, and perhaps could still be, if the power inherent in the human state to disassociate oneself from a situation (as if it were happening to oneself as an external experiencer) had not been used. They may be presentiments of possibilities of situations already implied in the present phase of the Movement of Wholeness, as a full-grown plant is implied in the germ seeking to pierce the crust of the soil and experience sunlight. Imagination can be, in other words, the activity of a mind having been impelled to enlist itself at the service of intuition so as to give substance and concreteness to the intuitive revelations. It performs this service if another faculty operates alongside the positive kind of image-making function: *faith*.

The word *faith*, however, is not used here in an ordinary religious sense, with reference to doctrines for which a specific divine origin is claimed. Faith rises in the consciousness which realizes that it is an aspect of Wholeness and that the whole meaning of any situation can never be revealed by the merely partial, local, and temporary interpretation the mind provides, nor by any desire which absolutely negates the value and meaning of its opposite. Faith implies an open approach to possibilities which are not included in the normal, natural response of the human organism as now developed on our planet, or which are not acceptable to the rational mind. Therefore, faith should not be considered to be mainly a product of a ritualized and/or institutionalized religious spirit. Human beings have faith in God and His revelation *because*, at the core of their whole being, they realize that the senses and (at a later stage of evolution) the objective, analytical, and rational mind do not—and indeed cannot—picture the wholeness of any being or any situation. The human person "intuitively" feels or realizes that the wholeness of whatever "is" includes more than he or she can be conscious of. This "more" can therefore be approached only through faith. Faith is the only possible approach not only to the non-rational and alogical, but to what the consciousness dimly feels to be beyond any sense-perceived reality.

As it performs such a function, faith should readily accept the cooperation of imagination. It must do so especially when it attempts to transform the cultural paradigms and the popular material interpretations of human experiences which the collective mind had to create in order to produce a sense of security in the satisfaction of basic desires that most people can share. A vivid faith that what is imagined can be concretely actualized is needed if the dream or utopia is to become a fact of human existence. When a religion postulates the existence of God as a changeless absolute Being whose nature and power are beyond the capacity for transformation of any limited and conditioned but evolving being, such a God can only be imitated. He or It absolutely transcends any conceivable mode of beingness. The theologian must therefore establish two categories of Beness, in metaphysics usually called "being" and "becoming." Man as a participant in be-coming can imitate and dimly reflect the divine state of timeless and immovable being, but no evolutionary process, no series of crises of transformation, can ever make Man (whether as an individual person, or as the whole of humanity) such a theologian's God. The only possibility is that of a "dialogue" between God and Man. This is a super-aristocratic type of situation: the good servant allowed to speak of his problems or doubts to the all-powerful and unfailingly wise king and master, whose voice sounds faintly through layers of veils.

The democratic image is, in contrast, that of the realizable American Dream: every newborn a potential big executive, or even the nation's President—the most powerful man in the world, it is believed. The sub-conscious (if not consciously admitted and entertained) faith in the validity of such a dream gives a quasi-mystical yet eminently effective power to the image of America. It has become, in the minds of billions of human beings, at least the prelude to a realizable utopia. The continual possibility of keeping active the drive to the ideal goal, however, requires the perpetuation (through educative processes and parental suggestion) of a quality of thinking, feeling, and behavior necessary for the effective actualization of the utopia. These requirements undoubtedly have produced an unparalleled sociopolitical and cultural situation; but collective moral restraints, already greatly weakened everywhere under the evolutionary pressure of the process of individualization, today are in a state of collapse. The traditional culture which made the unfoldment of the potentiality of individualized personhood relatively secure, through a step-by-step process with clearly defined transitions (rites of passage), has lost most of its structural and revelatory function. The only effective faith left is centered in the taken-for-granted feeling that "I" Peter or Jane can be anything I want as an ego in control of whatever situation I may personally face.

Nevertheless, in practically all cases such a situation has a social character: it involves relationships with other egos which—whether or not they admit and understand the fact—can be expected to cooperate if the situation is managed intelligently. This is the social way. It is also the way of the ego-mind because it is based on the desire for strictly individual existence, however closely life is shared and benefitted by an intimate association with persons within a permissive, loosely structured sociocultural system.

The only logical possibility in that system is majority rule, and the use of statistical computations and polls. These in turn lead to the demand for ever more inclusive and more private information, to uncontrollable publicity, and more or less extreme forms of brainwashing through the forever and everywhere active media. More faith-compelling images are needed, stimulating an irrational faith in an unlimited future. According to such a faith, the proliferation of material images will in time change the level of the human consciousness. It will do so apparently through the eventually unanimous realization that the development of a wonderful structure of interpersonal and international relations *can* arise from the recognition, *by every ego*, that its own subjective desires and personal interests can best be served by communication, consultation, vocal discussion from person to person, and compromise.

Today, this possibility seems a forlorn hope, though the social and political process involved in its realization is evidently partially valid. It is valid because, in terms of the Movement of Wholeness, it should be considered inevitable in an evolutionary sense. I am nevertheless trying to evoke a type of faith based on the realization that archetypal solutions are already formed and active to some degree, in some internal ego-transcending manner. It is a faith solidly rooted in a cyclic vision, and in the affirmation of "being" in all possible modes of actualization, whether predominantly objective or subjective. It is faith in and through which Wholeness asserts itself; and there is no level or situation in which Wholeness cannot assert itself. In such an assertion, however, Wholeness does not have to reduce the many-sided yearning for the experience of "beyond" to the concept of an incomprehensible, absolute, yet miraculously intervening God. In Wholeness, every phase of the cyclic motion follows, conditions, evokes, announces, and is transformed into another phase. Nothing is alien to anything; every possibility interacts with every other. Yet there is structural order, invariant and supreme, because Compassion and karma always balance and restore order to the variations aroused by the relative freedom of human desires and will. And this freedom is one of the aspects of cyclic being.

Grounded in such a faith, empowered by a will which focuses an emergent desire for self-renewal, mind can bring to a crisis of transformation the imaginative solution that reflects the archetypal reality of the individual's dharma. Yet an archetype is only a formula of relatedness; it is a structural, not an existential factor. A type of person, even more than a particular isolated individual, has to work out and make the formula explicit and concrete. This, however, demands as a prerequisite a process of severance from old solutions which have become obsolete and confining.

Severance, whether as a physical or mental process of disengagement, is nevertheless an individualized experience. It can only acquire an irrevocable character if the subject that seeks freedom has the courage totally to overcome an insistent bondage to past habits of feeling, thinking, and behavior. Disenthrallment requires courage—not only great, but sustained and persistent courage.

At the level of a relatively primitive culture, this courage is implanted in the consciousness by the Elders and the traditional behavior of the community. Had they not long ago stepped beyond the known through the hallowed if terrifying rite of passage, leading to what for them was still the yet-unknown? The candidate to Initiation could indeed find within his or her inner psychic being the faith that would sustain through the ordeal. He or she would never leave the sacred field of the tribe's collective psychism: there was no question of belonging or not belonging. The only issue was how well and courageously the series of steps was being taken.

At the level of the individualized person, who has to pass seemingly alone through the varied tests of overcoming which life itself now presents, a different, perhaps greater kind of courage has to be displayed. It demands an even stronger, almost unchallengeable faith in the reality of an individual Soul. Yet our modern religions, and especially our culture, have failed to give a clear understanding of the meaning and purpose of the crucial crisis-situation. What is the potentiality implied in a successful conclusion of the crisis? Where does this individual Soul belong, and how can it be defined in a realistic sense? A superior, because more inclusive, level of reality has to be accepted and intensely believed in. The person in crisis must insistently *want* to operate at that level, even if he or she cannot fully understand what it implies. At that level the Communion of transhuman Pleroma beings act and have their being. It is the "Commonsoul" of humanity. It is the Soul of the Earth-being.

The individual person who has passed successfully through the radical crisis of total transformation should come to realize that, in a realistic sense, his or her "Soul" is essentially a particular place and function within the vast field of activity and consciousness of the Earth-being. There is no incomprehensible mystery in that fact, even if it has to be understood at a more-than-human level of consciousness. The victorious individual not only comes clearly to "see" what that place and function within the planetary greater whole (the Earth-being) is and has always *potentially* been; he or she is ready to act and live as a responsible agent for this greater whole.

As this readiness begins to overcome the force of strictly individual desires, a higher form of courage, united with understanding and wisdom, should be gradually experienced. The pull of the place and function waiting to be filled by an individual person acts as the substance and potency of that courage. This courage has to be maintained as an unquestionable state of being. It may take many existential forms, but it always is basically the will to endure and unflinchingly face the ancient karma of failure, without apologies, regrets, or feelings of guilt. It has happened. It is part of the whole. It is being redeemed, and the discord is being justified in terms of the new tone-resonance it created, bringing forth a new aspect of the undefinable reality of Wholeness.

There is no problem in Wholeness, save the belief in problems. Therefore the issue is faith—the quality and inclusiveness of the faith. It must be the faith in the meaning and value of the most extreme polarities of being, of both Unity and Multiplicity. That meaning and value are embodied in the Supreme Person, for in this realization of the archetype of personhood, the two polarities of cyclic being are as completely realized as they can ever be.

Personhood is the Solution envisioned by the Godhead, yet it is not an end in itself, for in it the seed of the Godhead state is implied. That seed will germinate in and through various levels of Pleroma being—a hierarchy of levels and transcendences, a periodic series of crises and overcomings that may mean victory or defeat—both of which have their place, value, and meaning in Wholeness. At every level of being, an experience of Wholeness is possible, but the field the experience encompasses increases at every new level. New situations arise presenting new possibilities.

The issue is always threefold, involving what is desired, what power is available, and what processes mind can discover for the transformation. The basic obstacles are inertia and fear. The enemy is within. The spiritual life is a state of war, and personhood is the battlefield. The weapons are courage and understanding, and the faith that images of victory are irrefutable realities.

9

The "Dangerous Forties" in the Life-Cycle of Humanity

The speed of change

According to the generally accepted interpretation of recent archaeological and paleontological discoveries, the basic biological structure of what is now homo sapiens began to operate in the earth's biosphere several million years ago. As our modern archaeologists understand the prehistoric development of human races, the new evolutionary capacities inherent in this type of organization have been very slow to manifest. The number of human beings remained very small, and the tribes struggling with one another for survival on several continents did not differ greatly from animal societies. In the latter, a definite and often very strict kind of organization has always been at work, dominated by biological needs and the instincts required for their satisfaction; and various modes of communication should be considered real languages—the language needed and effective at the level of animal consciousness.

One of the most basic differences between the human and the animal stage of living and experience may have

213

revealed itself when human beings discovered the various uses of fire, particularly the possibility to use fire to transform materials so as to make them more satisfying. While all animals fear fire, human beings overcame this biologically rooted fear once they realized that the changes produced by fire could be not only welcome but deliberately used to improve human existence and generate a new form of power. After a forest fire, a nearly burnt animal may have shown the value of cooking living organisms, and perhaps the effects of extreme heat on pieces of matter on the ground may have suggested procedure which eventually led to the making of pots, bronze arrows, etc.

According to many religious and all occult traditions, however, the use of fire was actually *taught* by superior Beings, rather than discovered by ordinary men or women. But whether one scenario or another is considered believable, the picture generally accepted by the modern mind refers to a period of millions of years. During this time primitive societies succeeded one another until, some five to six thousand years ago, a clearly marked change occurred and a new type of social organization began to develop.

It is impossible to ascertain whether material changes in the conditions of life and new possibilities of inter-personal relationships impelled human beings to operate at a more complex, more differentiated and more inclusive level of organization, or whether the new societies took form because a sufficient number of people had experienced an inner "revolution in con-sciousness" affecting their personal and group approach to life and the world around them. The simplest answer is that the time had come for the drive toward a radical transformation to operate synchronously at both the societal and the personal-psychological (or psychic) levels, because a critical phase in the relationship of the principles of Unity and Multiplicity had been reached in the evolution of the whole planet.

The change was critical in the sense that it induced a crisis of transformation affecting all three basic aspects of human experience. It engendered new types of desires, new modes of energy (more societal than strictly biological), and new procedures for the actualization of the desires. These procedures were needed to cope with, interpret, and justify the subjective eagerness to handle, manage, and intellectually understand the operation of the new energies generated by the complex interpersonal and intergroup relationships developing in relatively large cities in which a centralized kind of power was becoming consolidated. The management of that centralizing power working on the products of human togetherness and social cooperation became the substance of politics and economics.

At the psychological-personal level, the centralizing process operates in the formation of an ego which, as we have seen, is the form taken by a human being's ability to adjust the relationships between the many drives of a human organism and complex societal situations in order to insure survival and the actualization of personal desires and ambitions. There are several points in history which should be seen as radical crises of all-human transformation: in ancient Greece, the rise of a rationalistic mind; at the same time in India the development in early Buddhism of an objective approach to the problems of human existence; then, 2,000 years later, European Humanism and the triumph of the empirical and analytical method of science. The changes in the thinking, the everyday activities and the feeling-responses of at least a minority of dynamic human beings representing the spearhead of human evolution have been far-reaching and presumably irreversible.

The speed at which they occurred gives them a startling character. Compared to the probable millions of years since the appearance of homo sapiens, the last five millenia, and especially the last two centuries, are mere seconds in the expectable life-span of a biological species. If we believe in the generally accepted Darwinian theory of evolution, what could have generated this sudden development of new or so far only latent mental faculties, and since the early Renaissance the nearly passionate urge to transform human living conditions by means of their application? Why did it not happen before? Was it the result of a basic change in the biosphere or the entire planet—a change more radical than a glacial period? Geologists do not usually base their calculations on some planetary event so far-reaching that it could have affected so rapidly and irrevocably the very foundation of the way in which the human species operates. Was then the relatively sudden change predicated in the structural development of the human organism?

We can indeed find a parallel to what the whole of humanity experienced at a historical level if we observe equally rapid periods of development during the life-span of one individual human being. These normal and expectable developments can help us more easily to understand the all-human historical process and what it is meant to achieve.

Crises of social and personal transformation

When a teenage boy or girl leaves a strictly religious family molded by traditions of the American South and suddenly finds himself or herself living in a very progressive university, the change can be shocking. The mind that fed mostly on Biblical imagery and beliefs suddenly has to assimilate materialistic and perhaps "far to the left" ideas. The shock can be even greater if, having shown unusual intelligence, a teenage youth from a traditional peasant European family has been sent by a wealthy American to study in the United States. Another kind of radical change may be experienced if a small-town lovely girl, working at a menial job, is courted by a rich man and marries him. Her latent mental faculties may rapidly develop as she faces an entirely different kind of interpersonal relationship.

In the life of most human beings a change involving both biological and psychological readjustment can be expected after what used to be called the mid-life period. This is the "change of life," also spoken of as the crisis of the forties, or the dangerous forties. In many instances, such a crisis precedes the biological menopause in women, and it is often experienced, in some perhaps less-overt manner, by men as well as women. An ego-type of subjective consciousness and desire which had become deeply involved in biological experiences (sex, child-bearing, nurturing, etc.) may more or less suddenly feel or imagine that the years of biological youth are nearly gone and that a deep-seated readjustment is imperative, whatever one's conditions of life (single or married, with or without children, etc.) have been for many years. The development of a somewhat new type of ego may be the answer to the new situation. In other cases, an attempt may be made to transcend altogether the ego level as it manifests in our present society, and to align one's consciousness with that of pioneers in the development of a new kind of interpersonal relationship and/or societal organization.

In ancient cultures in which the life-span of a human being was divided into quite sharply differentiated periods, each with a definite meaning and function, the

"change of life" after age forty often led to a basic altera-
tion in a person's activities and feeling-responses. From
a more modern psychological point of view, the change
may not have such definite outer social or family implications and expected consequences, but it should be
understood as a process of personal and psychic readjustment which to some extent polarizes what was
experienced at the time of puberty; thus I have spoken
of it as "adolescence in reverse." If the years surrounding puberty had involved a strong psychological or
psychic crisis, this crisis may have a more or less related
counterpart during the seven-year period from age
forty-two to forty-nine. These years may witness either
a tense, quite irrational and perhaps antisocial (or
asocial) reaction against the set patterns of family
and/or business which had dominated the twenties and
thirties, or a kind of resigned acceptance of the life
process. In the most positive cases, however, the crisis
may be made to serve a conscious and deliberate
process of transformation. The subjective desires and
mental images of achievement of the individual person
may be reoriented and made to resonate, however
feebly, to the tidal rhythm of the Movement of Wholeness.

This crisis of the forties in a person's life may be
significantly used to interpret in a broad and symbolic
sense a corresponding period of tense and crucial
readjustments in the long-term evolution of mankind.
We are today passing through such a period. By realiz-
ing what is implied in such a correspondence, we may
understand in depth, and no longer merely in terms of
superficial symptoms (wars and revolutions), what has
really taken place in the Western world, particularly
during the last centuries. Humanity is experiencing a
potentially drastic "change of life." It is experiencing it
because the Movement of Wholeness on this planet
has reached a new phase in the relationship of the

two great principles which structure the evolution of humanity.

The correspondence is evidently not obvious if we assume the validity of the today generally accepted Darwinian theory, and we think of biological and human evolution exclusively in material and biological terms. However, if we do, we cannot answer the crucial question: Why has the radical change in the state of human society, of human thinking, and lately of the balance of forces in the whole biosphere, been so sudden and spectacular after an immense period of relatively slow transformation over millions of years?

Two answers may be given to this question. The first involves the entire planet as it moves around the center of our galaxy: the earth may have moved into a region where strikingly new energies or subtle substances are active. The second answer implies that our present humanity is only one in a series of successive developments, each of which brings out a specific range of the vast possibilities contained in the archetype MAN. Humanity was born and has been growing through definite *age periods* which roughly correspond to childhood, adolescence, and training for mature biological and social activity, then productive maturity. Now a crisis of transition, the "change of life" is being experienced. It may (yet need not) lead to one or two new age-periods.

If, however, we relate the sequence of age-periods in the unfoldment of an individual person to that of the vast cycles of evolution of mankind as a whole, we have to deal not merely with the birth, development, and gradual disintegration of particular races and cultures, but with altogether different types of human civilizations on more or less definable continents. We are dealing with what the most well-known quasi-esoteric traditions of our time have named Lemuria and Atlantis, and with the present spread of continental masses. Each of these stages of continental formation and the type of human beings having operated and now operating on them corresponds to one basic age period. Humanity, as homo sapiens, was "born" on Lemuria and there experienced its childhood; its years of adolescence correspond to the Atlantean period. With the gradual disintegration of the Atlantean regions (which may have ended around 8000 B.C., but had already started several hundred thousand years before), our present humanity began. Its geographical "heart center" is traditionally located in central Asia (the mysterious and invisible Shambhala), but its entire field of operation encompasses Eurasiafrica and, presumably, its geomorphic polarity, the Americas.

The present phase of human evolution therefore corresponds, in a global sense, to the period of maturity in a person's life-span (in general, between age twenty-eight and forty-two). The crisis of the forties, which presumably began several millenia ago, when large cities were built and a new type of psychological responses and ego-ambitions developed, has reached a virulent state—particularly since the Renaissance, the growth of the scientific mentality, and the desires and expectations associated with the ideal of democracy and egalitarianism in all fields. Where the crisis will lead is evidently the most basic question one would want to be able to answer. Any answer, however, will be conditioned by the basic meaning one gives to the crisis; thus by the level at which one thinks and operates.

If the change is thought to refer primarily or essentially to the level of material productivity and socio-cultural and political developments, a tentative scenario for the future may be outlined. It may sound logical, but only if no spectacular cataclysm or all-out nuclear war occurs. One may also believe that the outer transformation of mankind implies, is caused by, or at least is synchronous with a fundamental change involving the way a person "feels-thinks" about himself or herself—a person's self-image in relation to his or her place in the universe, or to God. Then one is confronted with a very different set of possibilities. Beyond the external social and material changes, one may perceive the rhythmic unfoldment of a process of all-human planetary transformation, one phase of which is gradually closing and another opening.

Rapid as it may be in terms of geological time, the transition may nevertheless take several millenia of historical time to be completed. Whether it is successfully completed in the foreseeable future should not be considered certain. The Greek (or Greco-Roman) culture was assuredly not a complete success. Yet it produced lasting results. It fecundated the minds of the pioneers of the Renaissance who reacted against the overwhelming power of the Medieval Catholic Order which had tried in vain to reproduce, at a new religious level, the material successes of the Roman Empire. European "humanism" led to the spontaneous but violent individualism of the Renaissance, and the struggle between gradually solidified nation-states, recalling on a larger scale the wars between Mediterranean city-states. Yes, "success" is evident if evaluated in terms of technological achievements. Similarly, the forty-year-old businessman or professional may find himself or herself in a solid social position; but his teenage children may have been arrested for the possession of drugs and require psychiatric care, while his marriage may be collapsing in meaninglessness.

Our present international world may be considered successful in what it has attempted to achieve at the level of consciousness and material welfare. But racked as it is today by psychic as well as economic conflicts, it probably has not yet reached the climactic point at which it will have fully to meet the karma of disharmonic collective efforts which produced the Industrial and Electronic Revolutions with their rapid spread over the whole globe. Whether this karma is successfully met may depend on a more realistic and complete understanding not only of the meaning of this "crisis of the forties," but of the state of being which may be at least partially reached by humanity *if* its planetary dharma is fulfilled, and *if* it moves to a new level of consciousness and activity. Our problem is indeed to realize what is possible, however lengthy the process of actualization. We need an ideal to orient our efforts.

Such an orientation may be obtained in an unexpected way if we study and really understand what the ancient system of organization in India, the Laws of Manu, established as basic periods of development in a human life. The fundamental meanings of these periods have often been misunderstood, especially insofar as the two last ones are concerned. Throwing a somewhat new light upon them should illumine our present human problems even if what is suggested may hardly seem possible in present world conditions. Conditions, however, must change.

The Hindu stages of life

According to the traditional Hindu doctrines, the full natural life-span of a human being is normally divisible into four stages (*ashrama*): *brahmacharya, grihastha, vanaprastha,* and *sannyasa.* During the first stage, the child and adolescent develops his or her innate capacities as a member of homo sapiens and of a particular culture, family, and social class. This *brahmacharya* process is twofold: generic-biological and cultural-mental. It ends when the human being, having "come of age," marries and devotes all that he or she has built to the perpetuation of the sociocultural and religious order according to the function that his or her birth-situation has determined—the person's individual share in the karma of humanity.

During the second stage, *grihastha*, the mature being and the spiritual identity behind the physical embodiment are drawn into a series of organized productive activities, biological and sociocultural. These in most cases entangle the person in a web of desires and commitments—in sexual satisfaction, emotional attachments or repulsions, nurturing and educational activities, and a variety of "business" operations whose central motive is the accumulation of profit. That the drive for profit operates at all levels, even those generally assumed to be spiritual, is a fact many aspirants to "higher" stages of being often ignore. During this second life-stage *kama* (the power of binding generic and collective desires) dominates the consciousness.

The transition from this "householder" (*grihastha*) stage, intent on productivity and profit at whatever level it might be, to the third stage (*vanaprastha*) constitutes the basic "change of life." It implies a radical reversal of the polarization of consciousness, a change from extroversion to introversion, and a reorientation of the desires, motives, and essential character of one's activities. The timing of the change has been given as when a man can see the face of his newborn grandchild. In societies where marriages are usually early, this could mean the beginning of the forties. The grandfather is then expected to enter into a new kind of relationship predicated, at least in many cases, on leaving the family home, giving the direction of his business to his son, and retiring to the forest surrounding the village or town.*

This third stage of life is called the "forest-dweller"; but the term leads to a misunderstanding. While the forest-dweller may have given up his family home and his *personal* business or occupation to live in retirement in the simplest possible way, he is also able to participate in a non-personal manner in the affairs of the entire community. He may become part of the Council of Elders, or serve in whatever capacity his personal life has trained him for. He serves the Whole of which he sees himself a part, but *without remuneration*. He has given up the profit motive and (theoretically or gradually) the personal ambition motive. Thus the traditional keynote of this third life-stage has been "sacrifice."

However, we have to understand that any action totally dedicated to the service of a greater Whole without any desire for profit has a sacred character. It is consecrated. The process of consecration should result from an internal or introverted experience of the reality of the life and power of that greater Whole. It normally requires that the structure and purpose of the tradition on which the operation of the Whole is based be studied and understood in terms of principles. These may be symbolized in religious, theological allegories (as in the Hindu *puranas*), or presented in their more abstract, metaphysical forms. Such a consecrated activity which no desire for profit incites and sustains is transpersonal. It is activity *through* a person but "in the name of" a Whole of which the person not only knows himself or herself to be a functioning part, but has proven to others his ability to perform that function.

---

*In the ancient Brahmanical system no mention was made of the development of woman according to such a pattern of life-span.

A fourth life-stage may begin when even that condition of existence and level of consciousness are transcended. This is the state in which the *sannyasi* lives, moving over the land, beyond any attachment to any particular community, focusing wherever he or she goes what, for the traditional Hindu mind, is the light and love of the Supreme Being. Quite evidently, such a stage was, and is even more today, reserved for but a few rare human beings, women or men. In other cultures, such beings were said to have reached the Age of Wisdom which, in principle, was often related to the years after sixty.

When one deals with what is historically possible today for humanity as a whole, the transition toward such a fourth life-stage has to be considered a remote ideal. It refers to what H.P. Blavatsky evoked for a far distant future as "a humanity of Christs and Buddhas." Sri Aurobindo spoke of such an all-human stage as a "Gnostic humanity." Yet the situation mankind is now facing may be interpreted as foreshadowing the beginning of a crisis of transition which should eventually lead from the stage of productivity and profit to that of transpersonal service to the "universal Community of Mankind" (Thomas Jefferson's term). Such a transition may be successful, but it need not be. At the present time it certainly is proving difficult and dangerous. To think of it in terms derived from an old social and religious system may not help the situation. The extreme complexity of the interpersonal and international relationships acutely stressing the profit and success motives has brought to a critical, feverish pitch a restless drive for new types of thought and action. These are likely to demand palliatives and to produce antidotes along socially regressive lines. These in turn may incite violent revolutionary activities, adding new discords to a dangerously tense situation.

The ancient Hindu approach to the development of personhood and to one of the most basic crises this development may produce in a foreseeable future is certainly not to be considered a workable *global* solution; yet it could suggest the direction in which a rather unexpected possibility of transformation of the human situation may occur. It is at least a possibility open to individuals who have become aware of what is implied in the concept of "profit."

The ability to make a profit from an activity or process one has undertaken is not merely a concept dominating the collective mentality of any self-consciously democratic society, but in most instances it is an ever-present goal and a hoped for daily experience of the purpose of living in such a society. This ability to make a profit occupies a central position in a democratic culture because such a way of life is oriented toward "success," and success is evaluated in terms of increase in material possessions and/or social prestige and credit-worthiness. This in turn implies an individualistic approach to interpersonal relationships, and the attribution of a basic importance to the ego and its development in a family and school environment.

Service versus profit

An individualistic society is today a profit-oriented society, because the profit-motive is attached indelibly to the current concept of individualism and even of what is ambiguously called human rights. The individual is, as a matter of course, expected to make profits from his or her activities; and profits become the "possession" of the individual acquirer. To possess is an extension of to be; it is the proof of being, even if it refers only to the "possession" of a body. The use of the body brings profits to the being who, as an individual subject, "owns" that body—a source of potential energy. But the subject has to feel somehow separate from the object he possesses if he is intended to use it. Use is understood in terms of acquired profit to the person identifying with his or her central reality, the ego. The ego—I myself, Peter or Jane—is the central reality in a society still dominated by an eighteenth century kind of abstract individualism, because the ego's ability to make free choices is considered *the* essential factor in any truly human situation. The mention of "free choice," however, is quite meaningless, unless one states the *motive* for the choice, and what factor in the total human situation is intended to profit from the selection of a particular approach and practical strategy.

If the human situation as a whole is clearly and irreducibly centered around the goal of increase in power of an "I" whose mind operates basically, if not exclusively, in terms of profit and increase of power *over* one kind or another of external entities (things or persons), the social environment which permits or glorifies such a centering inevitably operates in terms of an individualism whose end-results can only be nefarious. At an early stage of the development of personhood, and as an effort to emerge from the psychic matrix of mother and family, this ego-type of individualism is presumably valuable. But the state of relatively autonomous and self-assured egocentricity to which it leads, *if* considered an end in itself and given an abstract and statistically measurable value, is inherently negative and the beginning of a *devolutionary* process.

The ancient Manu system of personal development was open-ended, for it gave a definable termination to the period of profit-making in an interpersonal, social context. The end was made biologically evident not only by the aging factor, but by the emergence of grandchildren. Similarly, according to the early Greek tradition, grandparents were (in a broadly human and evolutionary sense) re-embodied in their grandchildren. The evolutionary rhythm, however, was not reduced to the biological level because, at least in India, a fourth stage of life was possible—the totally open-ended *sannyasa ashrama*. There was no theoretical end to such a condition of being, except an undefined and indeed undefinable state of *samadhi*. At the *sannyasa* level even the thought of profit and social success could not appear. The *sannyasi's* way was based on the daily experience of total service, first to the village-community where he had religious as well as biological roots, then to any larger community that could be served, but served in a transcendent spiritual sense rather than in organizational communal terms.

What is to be meant today by the word *service*, which has been so deprived of real value in a human, personal sense, and mainly applied to complex machines—so complex indeed that they repeatedly require "service"? Can the word also be used with reference to the work of professionals or semi-professionals whose highly valued function today is to repair individual persons and help them to operate more smoothly in different interpersonal situations, or to deal successfully with crises of radical reorganization? An average person who has gone through the often intensely disturbing process of ego-differentiation and youthful self-assertion may indeed be considered (at least from a strictly psychological point of view) a complex psychic mechanism whose operations have been thrown out of balance by the disruptive pressures and unnatural demands of their environment. Service can also take the form of a special relation deliberately established by individuals who are self-dedicated to the attainment of a normality-transcending state of existence—a relationship linking them to more-than-human beings already operating in such a planetary, super-cultural, and transpersonal state.

In the past, a pre-democratic, pre-American, and now pre-electronic way of living often had a highly significant place for "servants" who belonged to a class socially inferior to the aristocracy of power, wealth, or mind. Service, in this sense, implied a "vertical" relationship, the less evolved or socially favored persons being related to individuals operating at a "higher" social level.* This relationship, however, could in principle function effectively and happily both ways, bringing indispensable benefits to both levels, though evidently servants were often abused, mistreated, and humiliated by the persons served. Nevertheless, unwholesome and degrading possibilities in the working out of vertical relationships should not give an intrinsically negative meaning to this type of relatedness. We should instead understand that at each level where vertical relationships operate, they assume a different character. The vertical relationship of cells to the whole biological organism in which they almost compulsively function differs in nature from the equally vertical relationship between a citizen and its government and police force, even in our egalitarian sociocultural system.

The principle of service is also given a new quality in the possible but as yet rarely actualized relatedness of an individual person to the Pleroma and, in a still

---

*The existence of vertical relationships according to a holarchic (rather than merely hierarchical) philosophy of being has been discussed in *Rhythm of Wholeness*, Part Four, chapter Twelve, p. 197.

broader sense, to the Earth-being as a whole. At these transpersonal levels also service has a realistic meaning only if substantiated in concrete situations. It does not merely refer to ideals having the diffuse emotional character of the common type of religious devotion. The transpersonal service relationship operates *through* the individually structured selfhood of a human person, but its motive is *beyond* the person. It is not pre-individual, as are many "religious" (or *bhakti*) feeling-responses, but individuality-transcending. The "Master" does not make personal demands of the "servant," because the former is no longer a person, but one of the two poles of a relationship whose essential purpose is the neutralization of karma. Any desire for, or even thought of, profit would negate not only the effectiveness but the reality of this kind of vertical service-relationship, because such a desire implies the inability to let go of the personhood frame of reference. The Pope calls himself "the Servant of the Servants of God"; but if what is being served is a *personal* God who demands tributes or sacrifices of one kind or another, the service-relationship is still pervaded with a feeling of profit, unconscious though it may be.

The making of profits can of course be the main aim of the activity of a collective person—a business corporation, a social class, a religious institution, or a nation. Where the profit-motive appears, in however subtle and pseudo-spiritual or altruistic a form, service is associated with productivity. The personally focused desire to produce results belongs, however, to the "householder" and, to a much lesser extent, to the forest-dweller stage. A true *sannyasi* no longer *desires* results. He or she is simply a wind of transformative power scattering seeds. The *sannyasi* serves the Movement of Wholeness. The Movement acts through him or her. Service, in that sense, is translucency. The true "server" is an unhindered beam of light. Beyond personhood and planethood, he or she reflects and to some degree embodies the quality of starhood, though the source of the stellar radiance may still be very remote and easily obscured.

The type of service implied in the third life-stage (*vanaprastha ashrama*), which theoretically follows the crisis of the forties, should not be understood solely as a vertical relationship, even though it involves the relation between a person and his or her whole community. The transition between the "householder" stage (oriented toward productivity and profit, and largely controlled by the ego) and the "forest-dweller" situation requires a readjustment of the horizontal relationship between the aging producer and the other members of his family and community. A non-ego-conditioned relationship from which the personal drive for profit and the desire to control the behavior of other people have been eliminated is still a horizontal relationship; nevertheless it moves in the direction of a new kind of achievement, that of a *consensus*. Competitors come to accept compromises. They may do so in terms of an extensive process of reorganization whose end-purpose may be the actual transcendence of the individualistic profit-motive.

As this motive is being transcended, another quality of relatedness is likely to emerge from the harmonizing of the separate ego-wills. The individual producers may realize their joint involvement in the economic and political health of the community in which, until then, they had operated with their own profit as the only goal. As this occurs, the individual accepts and comes to desire vertical relation to a greater whole, the community, more than any horizontal relationship.

This community, experienced at first as a physically objective reality, sooner or later may become not only a *psychic* field in which interacting personal desires still conflict, but an integral mental-spiritual organism. In due time this organism will be known as the Earth-being, and practically all limited relationships will be absorbed and transfigured into that one all-inclusive relation. Then the once conflicting ego-wills of self-assured individuals, having learned to achieve consensus, can function as distinct but centrally unified "agents" of the planetary whole in a condition of inter-penetration of consciousness.

At that stage consensus becomes unanimity. Individualized forms of consciousness interpenetrate. The participants not only "sense" (or feel) together; they realize that one "Soul" (*anima*) operates through their differentiated fields of being. Individual or group minds may differ as to policies and methods; but these differences chord into a total resonance in which the needs of each and all are met. They are met by being transcended in a deeply-felt acceptance of the karma, to the neutralization of which every different person contributes in his or her own way.

This unanimity state may be reached in limited groups or religious communities when what other people would call a utopia becomes, for the interpene-trating minds, a concretely perceived Presence and the effective fulfillment of a totally shared desire. But unless some drastic events occur which both radically alter the present conditions of life of mankind and enormously reduce the numbers of human beings, one can hardly think of this future stage as a practical possibility. Today, unanimity is most often totalitarianism in disguise.

To reach unanimity in any true and realistic sense, human individuals have to pass through the consensus stage which is now slowly developing. But even that stage is usually encumbered by the ghostly presence in memories of long-held individualistic opinions and egocentric profit-motives fighting crudely or surreptitiously for control of the group-situation. A significant and effective consensus is only reached when the situation being faced is felt to be of the utmost seriousness. What the consensus may reveal, however, is the unwillingness of the participants in the decision to interpret what is occurring as the indication that a radical change of attitude has become imperative.

Many human beings today are more or less clearly aware that such an indication is evidenced by the catastrophic possibilities inherent in the pollution and chemical transformation of the biosphere and stratosphere, as well as in the international war of nerves and the starvation of millions in many overpopulated and mismanaged countries. But many people, especially in developing countries, insist on believing that the Industrial and Electronic Revolutions are historical phases of a typically human kind of growth. They assume—and want to assume!—that the difficulties such phases have engendered can be solved without a basic reversal of personal or sociocultural attitudes. A thoroughly technologized and automated society moving faster and farther away from the archaic state of a primitive mankind bound to natural processes provides—they believe—the effective solution, if uncompromisingly applied. In their view, a worldwide consensus is undoubtedly needed, but we have all that is required to reach it if we keep talking, taking chances with unemployment, starvation, and limited wars, muddling through relatively small crises, and thereby avoiding the big crisis nobody wants to face or even less to understand.

According to the philosophy of Operative Wholeness,

as long as the linear ideal of "progress"—the nine-teenth-century god!—is not superseded by or inte-grated into a holarchic concept of rhythmic unfoldment, a crisis of reorientation of activity and revaluation of desires—a "change of life"—will be needed.

A vague psychic feeling of what is needed, not only for individual persons but for the whole of mankind, may be the unconscious or semiconscious cause of the recent publicity in the United States given to Christian "conversion" and "born again" experiences. Yet this emotional, sentimental "return to the Mother"—which does not seem greatly to alter either the everyday way of life and social ambition or the drive for personal and group profit of those having experienced it—has little to do with the transition between the Hindu "house-holder" and "forest-dweller" stages of life. What is needed is not a *return* to anything, but a basic shift in the frame of reference in which the ego and its profit-oriented mental processes operate. Such a shift occurs when the drive for productivity and profit—at the psychological as well as the material level—is replaced by an uncompromising readiness to serve the require-ments of the greater Whole, and to do so in terms of the most basic principles of organization the mind is able to understand and act upon.

Fundamentally, this greater Whole is *the human situa-tion* on the entire planet; but few persons are called upon or able to deal with it in terms of the complex interrelatedness of all the factors involved in it. The important point is not how large the scope of the pos-sible service and the field to which it can apply actually are. Rather, it is whether an individual human being believes himself or herself to be an essentially free and independent subject separate from the situation in which he or she is involved—or whether the person consciously and deliberately attempts to deal with it and all it implies as an operative whole. Does an "I" exist *outside* the total experience, or is not this "I" an intrinsic part of the situation—a part to which a confusing or illusory meaning is given if it is taken out of the complex interweaving of factors which, in their togetherness, constitute this situation?

This entire book refers to such a question, already posed in the first chapters. The answer being suggested is that the primary or essential reality of "being" is a cyclic series of interrelated whole situations, rather than a Gnostic drama of the Pilgrimage of an immense number of Souls. Such an answer, however, is only significant when it is made vibrant with a new approach to human experience. It is not sufficient to assent to it intellectually as a philosophical imperative. The change should be lived through in the depth of personhood.

The power of such experiences can and usually should be very profound and moving. It has to be met fully, unreservedly in all its consequences, as well as understood in its deepest roots. This requires not only a total commitment to all aspects of human experience. It demands a mature, courageous, long-sustained mind—the mind of wholeness.

It is always possible for anyone to take the first steps on the way of vertical relatedness to the Earth-being. These steps have to be taken in the concreteness of the opportunities and challenges of the state of personhood. We are all concrete persons. We are concrete individual solutions to ancient failures, reawakened as karma in the consciousness and activity of the Earth-being. But in the facing of this karma, what was at first only a karma-neutralizing possibility may engender the clear realization of the place and function that each autonomous human being, in his or her individual selfhood, already *potentially* occupies within the planetary Pleroma. This place and function is the individual Soul of the human being as it could operate within the whole planet's Commonsoul, thus fulfilling the archetype once created by Hierarchies of the divine Mind.

It *could* operate in this way. The place and function are here. The potentiality is present. Why does the process of actualization seem to require "so much time"? The reason is that it *is* time. It is the waiting. Yet, even more, it can be the doing—one step after another. We may refer to these steps as a series of lives, incarnations; but it is one process.

Of this process we, as embodied persons, should ask nothing. No profit is involved—only to "walk on" with the rhythm of the Movement of Wholeness beating within our heart and mind, peacefully, in uttermost simplicity. This rhythm may be difficult to hear, yet it can absorb the many raucous or exalting sounds of personal relationships into the vibrations of a silence in which Wholeness experiences itself, always and everywhere.

The crisis all human beings face is a crisis of belief. Ineluctably, crucially, even if imprecisely, one great question arises out of the challenges of one situation after another: what is *possible*? Sooner or later, anything is possible which a focused, resolute will starts without demanding of any situation that it, and no other, actualize the potentiality. The presence of Wholeness is implied always and everywhere, at whatever level of reality a whole situation operates. But it has to be the whole situation, not merely "I" assuming the role of the experiencer and asking for profit or "spiritual" growth.

Epilogue

In the immeasurable cycle of the Movement of Wholeness, a moment of supreme experience comes when, at the ever-present "meeting of the ways," the greatest Lord of Darkness challenges the most radiant Presence of Light. From the deepest regions of obscurity, the python of negative emptiness rises to the light, uncoiling its devastating power. And the combat rages.

There can be no end to the crucial embrace, no limits to the battlefield. For, while in his supreme effort the Lord of Darkness finds his vision confused by his hateful desire to annihilate light, in the sublime love of the radiant Presence, even the deepest darkness is always included.

There is no annihilating victory. Light and Darkness are one in an encounter that has neither beginning nor end. For Darkness can never see, and Light never ceases to love. Meaning forever rises out of the ubiquitous battlefield of Space in the eonic experience that is reality—always.

Index

239

These contemporary Quest books are also available—

ON REINCARNATION
The Cathars and Reincarnation—Arthur Guirdham
An English girl remembers her 13th century life as a heretic.

ON ASTROLOGY
Astrology of Transformation—Dane Rudhyar
A four-step approach to psychology through astrology.

ON HOLISTIC HEALING
Health: A Holistic Approach—D. Chernin &
G. Manteuffel
Two physicians incorporate homeopathy, nutrition, yoga, and
stress-therapy into the healing process.

ON YOGA
Yoga For a Better Life—David Schonfeld
With many illustrations. Complete with a chapter on how to
compose your own yoga course.

ON ESP
Exploring Psychic Phenomena—D. Scott Rogo
Heavily documented case-histories help provide a rationale
for ESP encounters.

Available from:
The Theosophical Publishing House
306 West Geneva Road
Wheaton, Illinois 60189

Phil Joppe

768 - 515 - 5994

aa   4^{15} a
269